STUDY GUIDE TO ACCOMPANY RUNYON, HABER, COLEMAN

BEHAVIORAL STATISTICS: THE CORE

STUDY GUIDE TO ACCOMPANY RUNYON, HABER, COLEMAN

BEHAVIORAL STATISTICS: THE CORE

Richard P. Runyon

McGraw-Hill, Inc.

New York St. Louis San Francisco Auckland
Bogotá Caracas Lisbon London Madrid
Mexico City Milan Montreal New Delhi
San Juan Singapore Sydney Tokyo Toronto

Study Guide to Accompany Runyon, Haber, Coleman:
BEHAVIORAL STATISTICS: THE CORE

This book is printed on acid-free paper.

4 5 6 7 8 9 0   DOC/DOC   9 0 9 8

P/N 054926-5
PART OF
ISBN 0-07-911433-4

The editors were Jane Vaicunas and Beth Kaufman;
the production supervisor was Elizabeth J. Strange.
The cover was designed by Keithley & Associates, Inc.
R. R. Donnelley & Sons Company was printer and binder.

Contents

Preface

PREFACE

Each chapter in the *Study Guide and Solutions Manual* corresponds to a chapter in the text *Behavioral Statistics: The Core*. The Study Guide has been designated to provide you with review and feedback concerning your mastery of the textual material. It is recommended that you study the assigned chapter thoroughly and complete the exercises in the text before proceeding to the Study Guide.

      Each chapter contains several different units. First, there is a statement of the behavioral objectives. If you achieve these behavioral objectives you have gone a long way toward mastering the fundamentals of statistical analysis. The statement of behavioral objectives is followed by a comprehensive chapter review that covers most of the important terms, symbols, concepts, and procedures undertaken in each chapter. Next there follows a series of multiple-choice items. This unit will provide you with an opportunity to practice taking exams. It may also serve as diagnostic items that reveal areas of weakness that require additional attention.

      It should be emphasized that the Study Guide is not intended as a substitute for the text but, rather, to serve as a supplement. If used in conjunction with the text, as recommended, the Study Guide should enhance your comprehension and enjoyment of the course.

Richard P. Runyon

1

Statistics: The Arithmetic of Uncertainty

Behavioral Objectives

1. Define statistics.
2. Define the terms commonly used in statistics.
3. Explain the goals of research.
4. Explain the Experimental methods.
5. Identify the role of statistical analysis in research.

What is statistics?

To begin with, many people have little knowledge of the formal aspects of the discipline called statistics but this does not mean that we are unable to behave in agreement with its many rules. For example, we may not recall how to calculate a proportion, but we do understand the statement, "A greater proportion of drunken than sober drivers have accidents that take lives or inflict critical injuries." It is accurate to say that our lives are broadly governed by our implicit grasp of statistical rules. Stated another way, we are statistically sophisticated living organisms.

In the first chapter of the text, we provided you with some of the formal procedures for collecting and analyzing data and making decisions or inferences based on these procedures. For example, you have been calculating proportions, percentages, and arithmetic means throughout most of your school years. If a baseball player has made 67 hits in 183 official times at bat, the proportion of hits equals $67/183 = 0.366$. The popular name for this statistic is batting average. If you obtained the following scores on five tests taken in a given course -- 83, 92. 73, 80, 96 -- you have little trouble calculating your average for that course. It is $(83 + 92 + 73 + 80 + 96) / 5 = 424/5 = 84.8$. You also know that an average near 85 is typically a grade of B.

What is research?

Research is directed at finding answers to important questions. Although many different techniques are involved, they share some important features in common.

1. Combining well-designed methods for obtaining answers (the research phase) with follow-up statistical analyses can reduce our uncertainty in a world of perplexity.

2. Successful research requires careful planning and accurately documenting attentive observations.

3. Research can take place in a variety of settings and be directed toward a diversity of problems.

4. Statistics are used to a) organize data b)summarize data and c) draw conclusions and make inferences from data.

Definitions of key terms frequently used in statistics

Data **Numbers or measurements that are collected as a result of observations.** These data are the keystone of subsequent statistical analyses.

Population **All members of a group of individuals, objects, or measurements that have at least one characteristic in common.** For example, during a national election, the population consists of all individuals in the nation who are qualified to vote.

Parameter **A value summarizing measurable characteristics of a population.** Parameters are rarely known but they can be estimated from a random sample (see next item).

Random sample **A subset of a population selected in such a way that each member or subgroup of that population has an equal opportunity to be selected.** A state lottery is an example of random sampling. If the population is 43 numbers and 6 are selected each week, the 6 numbers are selected at random.

Statistic **A summarizing value resulting from the manipulation of sample data according to specified procedures or rules (e.g., calculating the proportion, percentage, or mean of the sample data).** A statistic can be used to infer a vslur of s parameter. It is to a sample what a parameter is to a population.

Variable **Any characteristic of a person, environment, or** experimental situation that varies from person to person, environment to environment, or experimental situation to experimental situation.

Independent variable **The variable that is manipulated or examined (such as sex, personality) in order to determine its effects on or relationship with a dependent variable (next item).**

Dependent variable **One or more variables (e.g., some characteristic of behavior) that are being observed and measured in order to assess the effects of the independent variable.** In other words, it is a variable whose values are assumed to "depend" on another variable (the independent variable).

Random assignment **In a true experiment, subjects are selected at random from a study group and then they are assigned at random to two or more experimental conditions.** If the independent variable *nod* is thought to be a sleep-inducing compound, some of the subjects are randomly assigned to a group that receives *nod,* and the remaining subjects are randomly assigned to a group that does not receive *nod.* Subjects are not told which group they have been assigned to. The dependent variable is *sleep,* which is carefully measured by the researchers.

Intact groups **Preexisting groups of individuals who differ from one another in terms of one or more characteristics of interest.** Thus, we may speak of males and females, Republicans and Democrats, smokers and nonsmokers as distinct and intact groups, and the so-called independent variables consist of the different characteristics of interest, such as political party, smoking habits, and sex. When intact groups are used as the independent variable, the study is not a true experiment.

True experiment **Such a study does not involve a comparison of intact groups. Rather it irequires random assignment of subjects to the experimental conditions (the independent**

variable) so that the only systematic difference is the treatment assigned to them by the experimenter(s).

A comparison of an intact group study with a true experiment

In a series of studies summarized in *Science News* (*Vol* 143, 1993, 21, 334), the potential health risks of living in the proximity of or downwind from a hazardous-waste incinerator plant were evaluated. In one study, various aspects of the health of a number of people living within a distance of 1.5 miles of a hazardous-waste incinerator plant were compared to the same aspects of health of people living about 8 miles away. The independent variable was the living distance from the incinerator plant. Note, however, that the subjects were not assigned randomly to the two distances involved in the study. Thus, the subjects living at each distance from the plant represented intact groups. The dependent variable consisted of several health conditions studied in each group. The investigators found that, compared to people living 8 miles away from the hazardous-waste incinerator, those living 1.5 miles away suffered 9 times as much coughing and wheezing, 2.4 times as many neurological disorders, such as seizure and tremors, and 1.4 times as many neurological symptoms such as blackouts, and partial loss of coordination, and increase in tingling sensations.

Such results are often reported in the media as proof positive that hazardous-waste incinerator plants are dangerous to the health of those living near the plants. Although, this is quite possible, this investigation is *not a true experiment*. There are other uncontrolled factors that might contribute to the poor health of those living near the incinerator plant. Their family size may be greater and income less, thereby leaving fewer economic resources for available health services. They may be living in more crowded home conditions that may increase the spread of transmissible disorders. Perhaps many more subjects living nearby are directly employed in the hazardous-waste plant, possibly exposied directly to health risks other than the emission of stack by-products.

In much medical and psychological research, it is not

feasible to achieve the basic requirements of a true experiment, specifically assigning subjects randomly to the independent variable. How many people living in the general locale of the hazardous waste plant would voluntarily agree to be randomly assigned to living within 1.5 miles from the plant compared to at a distance of about 8 miles?

Table 1.1   Examples in which a true experiment will not be performed because of ethical, logical, or economic reasons

----

True Experiment Subjects randomly assigned to experimental conditions	**Intact Group Subjects al-already belong to the research condition and there is no random assignment**

Purpose: *To determine the effects of smoking (independent variable) on various aspects of health and/or behavior (dependent variables)*

Smoking conditions assigned to experimental subjects usually on some random basis. Control subjects are assigned to non-smoking conditions.	Subjects who are already smokers become the "experimental subjects." Nonsmokers become the control subjects.

Purpose: *To determine the effects of an illicit drug (independent variable) on cognitive tasks, psychomotor performance, and/or health (dependent variables)*

Illicit drugs are assigned to experimental subjects. Control subjects are assigned to non-drug conditions.	Subjects who are already illicit drug users become "experimental subjects." Nonusers become control subjects.

SELF-TEST: MULTIPLE CHOICE

Multiple-choice exercises will be included with every chapter of this Study Guide. After you have complete and scored each quiz, focus your attention on the items where you guessed correctly or answered incorrectly. Try to state, in your own words, why you incorrectly selected a given answer as correct.

1. The plan for collecting data is called the:

a) descriptive function   b) inferential function   c) research design   d) statistical analysis   e) random sampling

2. A characteristic of a population that may be measurable is:

a) statistic b) sample c) parameter   d) datum e) constant

3. A number resulting from the manipulation of raw data according to certain specified procedures is called a:

a) statistic   b) parameter c) sample   d) population
e) constant

4. In order to estimate the ratio of male to female students in a college, a professor decides to calculate the proportion of both males and females in one of his classes. The resulting proportions are:

a) statistics b) parameters c) constants   d) populations
e) samples

5. A national survey was conducted on 10,000 female and male adults to estimate the proportion of female voters, The individuals surveyed represent a:

a) population b) parameter c) statistic d) data e) sample

6. In Exercise 5, the 10,000 subjects:

(a) belong to two different experimental groups b) represent dependent variables c) represent intact groups d) all of the above (e) none of the above

7. To study the effects of food deprivation on activity, subjects are deprived of food for a period of 10 hours. This time of deprivation is a(n):

a) independent variable   b) random sample   c) dependent variable   e) parameter

8. In Exercise 7, the activity measure is a(n):

a) independent variable   b) intact group   c) dependent variable   e) descriptive statistic   f) inferential statistic

9. In inferential statistics, the purpose is often to make inferences about _____that are based on _____ taken from the _____.

a) samples, populations, samples b) statistics, samples, populations c) statistics, populations, samples   d) populations, samples, populations e) samples, statistics, populations

10. When a television rating service reports that 100 million people watched a National Basketball Association championship game, the statement represents:

a) a wild guess   b)   the number in the sample   c) the known population d) the parameter e) an inference from a sample

11. If we wish to know if the values of two variables go together, our focus is on:

a) correlation   b) statistical inference c) a population d) a survey   e) a parameter

12. Which of the following is the correct use of the term "statistics"?

a) Martha bench-pressed 325 pounds.   b)   Speaking of statistics, our firm sold one coat worth $43,500 last week. c) At Ybrik University, Ray is just one more statistic. d) The annual per capita cost of educating a student at Ybrik University is $22,000.

13. A study compared the academic motivation of two groups of students, those who were doing drugs with those who are not. This type of study is:

a) correlational   b) a true experiment   c) an intact group study d) random assignment e) none of the above

14. A characteristic of a person, environment, or experimental situation that may take on different values is referred to as:

a) constant   b)   data   c) population d)   variable e) parameter

15. In statistics, Greek letters are commonly used to represent:

a) samples b) statistics c) data d) parameters e) variables

16. In performing the descriptive function, behavioral scientists:

a) make broad inferences about populations based on sample statistics
b) determine whether or not there has been an effect of the independent variable on experimental subjects
c) focus their inquiry on estimating values of parameters
d) all of the preceding
e) none of the preceding

17. Measurement of four individuals reveals their weight to be, in pounds, 120, 220, 185, and 147. These numbers represent:

a) data b) statistics c) variables d) parameters e) samples

18. A scientist investigating the effects of environmental temperature on the rate of chirping among crickets in a given locale must draw the sample from the population of:

a) all chirping insects b) arctic and tropical crickets c) crickets in the region of study   d)   noncrickets as well as crickets   e)   the different sounds that crickets make

19. In Exercise 18, the independent variable is:

a) crickets   b) rate of chirping   c) all sounds made by crickets d) the locale of the study   e)   environmental temperature

20. In Exercise 18, the dependent variable is:

a) crickets   b)   chirping sounds made by crickets c) all sounds made by crickets   d)   the time of the year e) environmental temperature

21. In performing the inferential function, behavioral scientists:

a)   make broad inferences about populations based on sample statistics   b)   determine whether or not there has been an effect of the independent variable on experimental subjects c) focus their inquiry on estimating values of parameters d) all of the above   e)   none of the above

22. Which of the following is *not* a variable?

a) a person's weight b) the number of feet in a mile   c) a friend's blood pressure d) the gender of a random sample of   subjects e) daily rainfall

23.   Which of the following is *not* an intact group?

a) students enrolled in a given course b) those who smoke two or more packs of cigarettes a day c) individuals assigned at random to a specific condition in a research study d) individuals placed in a research condition on the basis of their high levels of intelligence   e) a study comparing the effects of alcohol on conceptual thinking of those who are heavy versus those who are light consumers of alcoholic beverages

24. Which of the following is *not* likely to be an independent variable?

a) *reaction time* to a sound stimulus b) the *amount of reward* following a correct response   c)   the *noise level*   in an experimental setting   d)   *physiological measures* following 10 minutes on a tread mill e) the *emotional reaction* to viewing a film containing high levels of violence

25.   Random assignment is used in:

a) intact group studies   b) selecting the independent variable c) selecting   the   dependent   variable d) true experiments   e) selecting the population for study

26. A census involves:

a) random selection from a population   b) the study of an entire population   c) an intensive investigation of a sample d) gathering sample data   e)   calculating statistics, such as the average

27. Behavioral research requires;

a) planning an investigation   b) deciding upon the correct statistical analyses   c) collecting data d) analyzing the data e) all of the preceding

28. The end product of many research efforts often includes:

a)   selection of an independent variable b) selection of a dependent variable c) selection of research design   d) handling masses of data   e) none of the above

29. An inadequacy of an intact group design is that:

a) it does not establish a cause and effect relationship b)   the subjects are randomly assigned to the experimental conditions

c) the independent variable is manipulated by the experimenter
d) the dependent variable is difficult to identify   e) none of the
above

Answers: (1) c; (2) c; (3) a; (4) a; (5) b; (6) c; (7) a; (8) c;
(9) d; (10) c; (11) a; (12) d; (13) c; (14) d; (15) d; (16) e;
(17) a; (18) c; (19) e; (20) b; (21) d; (22) b; (23) c;   (24) a;
(25) d; (26) b; (27) e; (28) d; (29) a

2

Basic Concepts

Behavioral   Objectives

1. Define mathematical nouns, adjectives, and verbs, and identify examples of each.

2. State the summation rule and the various generalizations that are based on these rules.

3. Distinguish among the three types of numerical scales, citing the three ways in which the scales may be used.

4. Define and distinguish among the nominal, ordinal, and interval / ratio scales of measurement. Find ways to illustrate the differences among these scales.

5. Describe the difference between discrete and continuous scales. Explain the types of errors that are commonly associated with each.

6. List the rules of rounding and apply them to real sets of data.

7. Distinguish among ratios, frequencies, proportions, and percentages. Convert percentages to proportions and vice versa.

8. Calculate proportions and percentages of frequency data that are classified into two nominal categories down the column, across the rows, and in terms of totals.

Chapter Review

Our species makes profuse use of symbols in virtually all aspects of communication. All things that surround us assume meanings beyond their mere presence. A slab of granite can be a memorial to a loved one and the symbol for a number can represent a quantity. The number and the granite are symbols.

Just as we must know words and the rules for their use (their grammar) in order to communicate ideas, we must know the symbols and the grammar of mathematics in order to communicate statistical concepts. Like written and spoken language, mathematics has nouns, adjectives, verbs, and adverbs. For example, "X" and "Y" are often used as nouns identifying a variable, representing quantity, scores, or values of a variable. Suppose you are conducting a study in which two variables are body temperature and the hours since last food intake. You might identify these variables as X and Y respectively. These symbols would be mathematical nouns.

Another noun often used in statistics is "N," which stands for the number of subjects, scores, or quantities with which you are dealing. If you had the following scores – 20, 35, 14, 5, and 16 – you could write the sentence N = 5, in which both N and 5 are nouns and the equal sign is comparable to the verb "is." In other words, N = 5 or N is 5.

Subscripts are mathematical adjectives that modify or give more precise information about the nouns they modify. In the series X_a, Y_8, N_2, the subscripts a, 8, and 2 are adjectives modifying the nouns X, Y, and N.

Just as the word "grow" is a verb in English, the symbols +, $\sqrt{}$, Σ, and ÷ are verbs in the language of statistics. They instruct the reader to perform such operations as add, extract the square root, sum a series of quantities, and divide.

Finally, there are adverbs in statistics that modify the verb as in written and spoken language. In the notation

$$\sum_{i=7}^{9} X_i =$$

X is a noun, Σ is a verb, i is an adjective, and i = 7 and 9 are adverbs that modify the verb Σ. The entire expression reads as follows: sum all the values of X from i =7 through the 9th value. In other words, add together $X_7 + X_8 + X_9$ or $\Sigma(X_7, X_8, X_9)$.

Numbers are commonly used in one of three different ways: to name or identify, to represent position in an ordered series, or to represent quantity (how much).

When a number is used to name or identify, the category

of numbers to which it belongs is referred to as a nominal scale of measurement. Examples include your social security number, post office ZIP, and uniform number if you engage in organized sports. The intent of a nominal scale of measurement is to identify and classify individuals or objects that have some characteristic in common. All individuals with a common ZIP number live within the limits of a specific geographical region.

The classifications within an ordinal scale indicate the position in an ordered series. Ranks are commonly assigned to individuals and/or objects on order to locate their relative position in an ordinal scale. Thus, the highest-ranking violinist in a symphony orchestra occupies the first chair whereas the seventh ranking violinist occupies the seventh chair. Note that these rankings do not have arithmetic properties. It would not be correct to claim that the difference in ability between the violinists occupying the first and second chairs is the same as the difference between the violinists occupy the sixth and seventh chairs.

The highest scales of measurement are the interval and ratio scales. By definition, the numerical values that are associated with these two scales are quantitative, permitting the use of such arithmetic properties as addition, subtraction, multiplication, and division. One major difference between the scales lies in the location of the zero point. In an interval scale, the value "zero" is arbitrary and does not indicate the absence of the quantity being measured. A temperature of 100 degrees in Arizona does not represent twice as high a temperature as 50 degree in Minnesota. In a ratio scale, there is a true zero point. It would be correct to say that a person weight 240 pounds is twice as heavy as another weighing 120 pounds.

There is another way of categorizing quantitative variables, that is, as discrete or continuous. Between values of a discrete variable, there are gaps that contain no values of the variable. The values of a discrete variable are typically, but not necessarily, whole numbers. Consider variables such as the number of transistors in a microchip, family size, or the number of items correctly answered on a multiple choice test.

However, an infinite number of intermediate values occur with continuous scales of measurement. Time, length, and weight are continuous scales. If you ask a few friends their heights and weights, they will probably respond with whole numbers, (e.g. 63 inches tall and 128 pounds or 74 inches and 230 pounds). These are approximations. On a very accurate scale, the 128 pounds may be 128.056672 pounds. A more accurate scale may yield a weight of 128.0566720234. Even this weight is an approximation since more accurate scales would yield values to a greater number of decimal places.

When reporting values derived from a continuous scale, we often need to round off the values obtained. Moreover, when dividing one value of a variable by another, we are frequently left with a remainder that extends infinitely to the right of the decimal point. For example, $1/3 = 0.3333333+$ and $2/3 = 0.6666666+$. In the accompanying text, we usually carry all answers to three or more decimal places than were in the original data and round off to two places. Thus, if your original data were in whole numbers, you would carry your answers to three decimal places and round to two.

Frequencies, proportions, and percentages

The above are three more concepts that are often used in statistics. *Frequency* is no more than a count of items, scores, objects or whatever is being measured. If 350 pinto beans out of a batch of 10,000 are discarded as unusable, the frequency of bad beans in this sample is 350. The proportion is merely the number of unusable items to the total number of beans in the sample, Thus, the proportion equals:

proportion of bad beans =   350/10000 = 0.035

To obtain the corresponding percentage, multiply the proportion by 100, Thus,

percentage = proportion X 100 = 0.035 X 100 = 3.5%

 or an average of three and a half unusable beans in the entire batch of beans or 3.5 beans, on average, per 100 beans.

In the behavioral sciences, it is not uncommon to obtain

from each subject measurements on two or more variables, which are then displayed in tabular form. To illustrate, information on two variables are displayed: *blood alcohol concentrations* and *age*. Table 2.1 displays this information for 839 unintentional drowning in North Carolina between the years 1980 and 1984 inclusive.

Table 2.1 Blood alcohol concentration (BAC)

Age	Less than 100 mg%	Greater than 100 mg%*	Row Totals
0 to 14	86	1	87
15 to 29	254	120	374
30 to 44	85	84	169
45 to 59	69	50	119
≥ 60	62	28	90
Column Totals	556	283	839

* The legal level of intoxication in North Carolina
Source: Morbidity and Mortality Weekly Report (1986, **35**, (#40), 635

As can be seen, the greatest number of high BAC mortalities was in the 15 to 19 age group (N = 120). However, this was also the age group with the highest number of drowning deaths in both the high and low-BAC concentrations. If we want to know the age group with the highest percentage of high BAC deaths for their total number, we look at the percentages across each age group. For example, the percentage of high BAC deaths among those drowning in the 0 to 14 group can be found by dividing 1 by 87 and multiplying by 100. This percentage equals 1/87 X 100 = 0.01149 X 100 = 1.15. This is a very low percentage of BAC related deaths.

Table 2.2 shows the low BAC and high BAC drownings for each age group expressed as percentages.

Table 2.2   Percentages of drownings related to low and high BACs among those in five age groups

Age	BAC less than 100 mg%	BAC greater than 100 mg%*	Row totals
0 to 14	98.85	1.15	87
15 to 29	67.91	32.09	374
30 to 44	50.30	49.70	169
45 to 59	57.98	40.02	119
≥ 60	69.89	31.11	90
Column Totals	**556**	**283**	**839**

* The legal level of intoxication in North Carolina

Looking at the summaries in Tables 2.1 and 2.2, it becomes immediately clear that the greatest number of drowning deaths as well as the greatest percentage of high BAC drowning deaths were in the age 15 to 29 group.

A third type of table involves the column percentages. For example, if you want to know which age group had the highest percentage of drownings in either the low or high BAC group, you divide the number in each age category by the column total and multiply by 100. These percentages are shown in Table 2.3.

Putting the three tables together, it is apparent that the 15 to 29 age group was at the greatest risk of drowning in North Carolina during the years 1980 through 1984.   The greatest number of total drownings were in this age group, as were the percentages across each age group.   Finally, the column percentages of drowning were highest in this group for both low and high BAC findings.

Table 2.3 Percentage of drownings in five age groups in which there were low and high BAC levels

Age	BAC less than 100 mg%	BAC greater than 100 mg%*	Row totals
0 to 14	15.47	0.35	87
15 to 29	45.68	42.40	374
30 to 44	15.29	29.68	169
45 to 59	12.41	17.67	119
≥ 60	11.15	9.89	90
Column Totals	(100%) 556	(99.99%) 283	839

Selected Exercises

I. Addition and Subtraction

Obtain the sum of the following:

1. +9	2. -18	3. +2.35	4. $(9 - 2) + (4 - 4)$
-7	-5	+1.16	
+2	+16	-5.13	
-5	+ 10	+4.33	5. 6.354 - 2.990
-6	-3	-3.19	

Subtract the second number from the first in each of the following:

6. 0.5467	7. 7.235	8. 26.03	9. 15	10. -16
0.2349	12.245	32.15	-26	-11

11. 0 .0090
    - 0 .9910

Multiplication

Calculate the product for each of the following:

12. 16.4
    8.2

13. 0.051
    -1.613

14. 11.2
    11.2

15. 44.59
    0.06

16. -2.25
    1.76

17. -0.01
    -0.01

Division

18. $14 \div 4$

19. $4.56 \div 2.28$

20. $(7-4) \div 1.96$

21. $15 \div -45$

22. $0 \div 5.5$

23. $-12 \div -12$

24. $-8 \div 2.5$

25. $.0066 \div .0022$

26. $15.3131 \div 5.5$

Summation rules

27. Find $\displaystyle\sum_{i=4}^{5} (X_i)$ when $X_1 = 4$, $X_2 = 5$, $X_3 = 6$, $X_4 = 7$, $X_5 =$

    and $X_6 = 9$

28. a. Find $\displaystyle\sum_{i=1}^{N} (X_i) =$ for the values given in Exercise 27.

    b. Find $\sum X^2$ for all the values given in Exercise 27.

    c. Find $(\sum X)^2$ for the values given in Exercise 27.

Equations Involving Fractions

29. Solve $a = b/c$ for b when $a = 6$ and $c = 5$.

30. Solve $\overline{X} = \sum X/N$ for $\sum X$.

31. Solve Exercise 30 for N.

32. Solve $\overline{X} = a + bY$ when a = 5, b = 1.5, and Y = 12.

33. Solve Exercise 32 for b when a = 5, Y = 12, and $\overline{X}$ = 12.

34. Find the value of SS when SS = $\sum X^2$ - $(\sum X)^2/N$ when $\sum(X^2)$ = 97.4206, $\sum X$ = 72.86 and N = 85.

Complex Operations

Perform the indicated operations:

35. $28/\sqrt{16}$ 36. $9\sqrt{144}$ 37. $4 \div 5^2$ 38. $(6 - 7 + 5)/5$
39. $(6 + 3) \div 3$ 40. $68 - 144/44$ 41. $20 - (10)^2 / 10$

Answers

1) -7;   2) 0;   3) -0.48;   4) 7;   5) 3.364 6) 0.3118 7) -5.010
8)   -6.12;   9)   41;   10)   -5;   11)   1;   12)   134.48;
13) -0.08313; 14) 125.44;   15)   2.6754;   16) -3.96;
17) 0.0001; 18) 3.5;   19) 2;   20) 1.53061;   21) -0.3333;
22) 0; 23) 1; 24) -3.2; 25) 3; 26) 2.7842; 27) 17;
28) a. 33   b. 271   c. 900;   29) 30;   30) $\sum X = N\overline{X}$;
31) N = $\sum X/\overline{X}$; 32) .23; 33) 0.5833; 34) 34.9667;   35) 7;
36) 108;   37) 0.16; 38) .8; 39) 3; 40) 64.72727; 41) 10

SELF-TEST: MULTIPLE CHOICE

1. Grouping individuals into low, middle, and high categories implies which type of scale?

 a) nominal b) ordinal c) interval   d) ratio e) continuous

2. Body height is measured on what type of scale?

a) nominal b) ordinal c) interval   d) ratio e) discrete

3. The symbol N, representing the number of observations, is a mathematical:

 a) verb b) adjective c) adverb d) noun e) predicate

4. The summation sign Σ is a mathematical:

 a) verb b) adjective c) adverb d) noun e) predicate

5. The scale characterized by the classification of events, objects, or persons which have no quantitative properties is called:

a) nominal b) ordinal c) interval d) ratio e) none of these

6. When someone says that Mary appears smarter than Susan, the scale of measurement is:

a) nominal b) ordinal c) interval   d) ratio e) standard

7. A truly quantitative variable with an arbitrary zero point is called:

a) interval   b) ordinal   c) standard d) ratio e) nominal

8. An example of a nominal scale is:

a) weight
b) order of finish of the teams in the NCAA women's basketball finals
c) the apparent size of an object
d) candidates for political office
e) socioeconomic status

9. The data employed with interval or ratio scales are frequently:

a) head counts   b) scores   c) ordinal position d) rank   e) none of the above

10. The lowest scale of measurement is:
a) ratio b) interval c) nominal d) ordinal e) discrete

11. Which of the following represents the highest order of measurement?

a) order of finish in a horse race b) male versus female c) temperature of Fahrenheit scale d)   length in inches e) selection of most popular instructor

12. The data employed with nominal scales consist of: a)   relative position in an ordered series   b) scores c) variables d) continuous numbers   e) frequency counts

13. The scale of measurement that is characterized in terms   of the algebra of inequalities is:

a) ordinal b) interval c) numeral d) nominal d) ratio

14. Variables in which measurement is always approximate because of an unlimited number of intermediate values are:

a) nominal b) discrete c) ordinal d) continuous d) interval

15. What are the true limits of 12.4 pounds?

a) 12.4 - 12.5 b) 12 - 13 c) 12.35 - 12.45 d) 11.5 - 12.5
12.3 - 12.5

16. The number 15.00500 rounded to the second decimal place is:

a) 15.00 b) 15.01 c) 16.00   d) 15.005 e) 15.05

17. What number has, as its true limits, 16.55 - 16.65?

a) 16.5 b) 16 c) 16.575 d) 16.625 e) none of these

18. The number 43.5499 rounded to the second decimal place is:

a) 43.54 b) 43.60   c) 44.00 d) 43.55   e) none of these

19. The number in the above exercise, rounded to the first decimal place, is:

a) 43.6   b) 43.4 c) 43.5 d) 44.0   e) none of these

20. The data used with interval or ratio scales are frequently referred to as:

a) head counts   b) scores c) ordinal position d)   ranks
e)   none of the preceding

Answers: 1) b; (2) d; 3) d; 4) a; 5) a; 6) b; 7) a; 8) d;
9) b;   10) c; 11) d; 12) e; 13) a; 14) d;   15) c; (16) a; (17) a;
18) d; 19) c; (20) b

Problem: Comparison of choline levels in nursing mothers in Ecuador and Boston, United States. (Zeisel;   R.J. Stanbury; J.B. Wurtman; M. Brigida; R.Fierro-Bemitez. "Choline Content of mother's milk in Ecuador and Boston." *New England Journal of Medicine*, 1982, Vol. 306. No. 3, 175)

A deficiency of choline (a B-complex vitamin) in the diets of laboratory animals leads to disorders of the liver, kidneys, and memory. It is suspected as a factor in similar disorders in human infants. Intellectual deficits and short stature are common among villagers in highland communities in Ecuador. Their diets appear to be low in choline. The following table shows a comparison of two samples of choline levels in nursing mothers in Ecuador and Boston.

Milk choline levels	Ecuador	Boston
0 to under 100	22	0
100 to under 200	15	3
200 to under 300	15	2
≥ 300	3	6

1. Prepare a table of the percentages of choline levels of mothers in Ecuador and in Boston.

2. Does there appear to be differences in the percentages in each sample?

3. Does this study qualify as a true experiment?

Answers

1.

Milk choline levels	Ecuador %	Boston %
0 to under 100	40	0.0
100 to under 200	27.3	27.3
200 to under 300	27.3	18.2
≥ 300	5.5	54.5
Column percentage	100.1*	100
Sample size	55	11

* Slight rounding error

2. Although the Boston sample is small, a high percentage of nursing mothers in Ecuador have low choline levels in their milk.

3. No. The subjects have not been randomly assigned to Ecuador and Boston. The study involves *intact groups.*

The   topic of graphs do not come up until Chapter 3. However, a *histogram* of data is presented at this point to show the value of a graphic device. It is immediately apparent that the choline levels of mother's milk in Ecuador is much different than among mothers in Boston.   The lowest   levels of choline in mother's milk is found in Ecuador   (40% of mothers) and the highest percentages is found in Boston(55%).

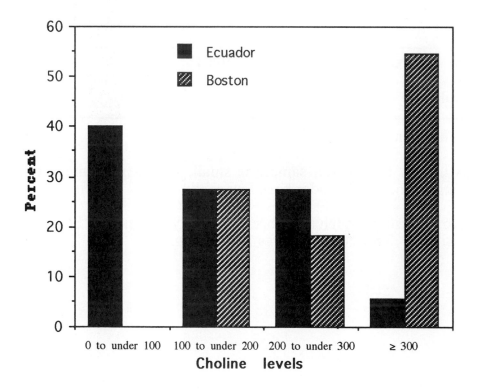

3

Frequency Distributions and Graphing Techniques

Behavioral Objectives

1. State the purpose and the procedures for organizing data into a frequency distribution.
2. Know the procedures for constructing a cumulative frequency distribution and estimating the frequency rank of a score.
3. Find the score corresponding to a given frequency rank
4. Know how to construct and interpret a grouped frequency distribution
5. Know how to construct a stem and leaf display of grouped data
6. Know how to graph and to construct different frequency distributions

Chapter Review

Twenty subjects filled out a questionnaire that sought their emotional reaction to a recently released film. Their scores on the horror scale are shown in Table 3.1. The higher the score, the stronger was their emotional reaction to the horror scenes.

The raw scores are shown below.

42	30	26	33	40
37	31	32	37	30
37	31	43	45	43
36	44	38	41	38

The next step is to arrange these scores from highest to lowest into a frequency distribution (see Table 3.1).

Table 3.1 Emotional reactions of 20 randomly selected movie patrons to a recently released film. The higher a score, the stronger was the fear reaction.

Score	Frequency
45	1
44	1
43	2
42	1
41	1
40	1
39	0
38	2
37	3
36	1
35	0
34	0
33	1
32	1
31	2
30	2
29	0
28	0
27	0
26	1
N =	20

Note that the highest score is 45 and the lowest is 27. Also, some scores have 0 as an associated frequency. The sum of all the frequencies is equal to 20. We can estimate the middle score (the 50th percentile) by counting either up or down 10 in the frequency column. Note that both counts end up opposite a score of 37. Although not precise, our estimate of 37 is a good approximation. Similarly, you can come close to a score at the 25th by multiplying N by 0.25 and counting up from the bottom. Thus, 20 X .25 = 5. The fifth frequency up from the bottom is 30. Similarly a score of about 41 is at the 75th percentile.

Table 3.2 extends the frequency distribution to the cumulative frequency distribution. You simply add the numbers in the frequency column upward from 1 through 45. Note that the last value equals N.

Table 3.2 Cumulative frequency distribution of the frequency column in Table 3.1

Score	Frequency	Cum f
45	1	20
44	1	19
43	2	18
42	1	16
41	1	15
40	1	14
39	0	13
38	2	13
37	3	11
36	1	8
35	0	7
34	0	7
33	1	7
32	1	6
31	2	5
30	2	3
29	0	1
28	0	1
27	0	1
<u>26</u>	<u>1</u>	1
	N = 20	

If you want to estimate the percentile rank of a score of 32, you divide the cumulative frequency associated with 32 (i.e., 6) and multiply by 100. Thus, cumulative percentage of a score of 32 equals 6/20 X 100 = 30th percentile. Similarly, the percentile

rank of a score of 40 equals 14/20 X 100 = 70th percentile.
    Finally, we divide each value in the cumulative frequency
column by N and multiply by 100 to obtain the percentage
cumulative frequency.

**Table 3.3 Cumulative percentage distribution based on the
cumulative frequency column in Table 3.2**

Score	Frequency	Cumf	Cum%age
45	1	20	100
44	1	19	95
43	2	18	90
42	1	16	80
41	1	15	75
40	1	14	70
39	0	13	65
38	2	13	65
37	3	11	55
36	1	8	40
35	0	7	35
34	0	7	35
33	1	7	35
32	1	6	30
31	2	5	25
30	2	3	15
29	0	1	5
28	0	1	5
27	0	1	5
26	1	1	5

N =   20

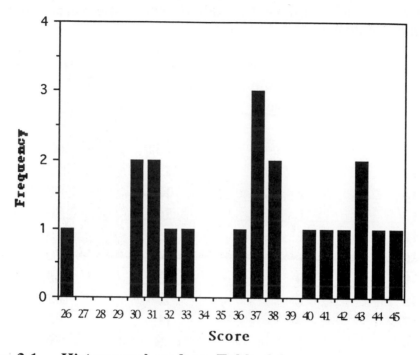

Figure 3.1   Histogram based on Table 3.1

Notice how well this graphic device displays the raw data. We have gone from a mass of unordered raw data to a coherent frequency distribution to a picture which has been credited with the "worth of a thousand words."

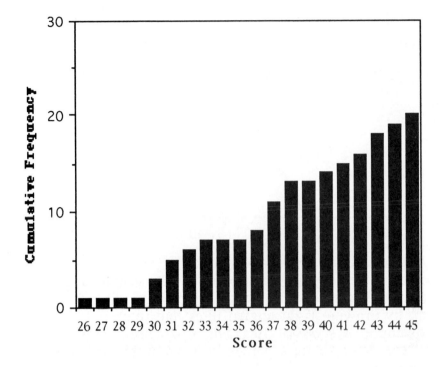

Figure 3.2   Cumulative frequency graph based on Table 3.2

The cumulative frequency graph shows the growth trends over all the scores obtained in this study. Notice that there is relatively little growth at both ends of the distribution with greater growth in the middle.

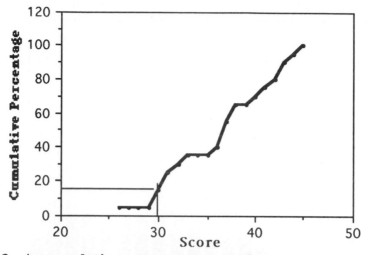

Figure 3.3   **A cumulative percentage graph**

Figure 3.3   A cumulative percentage graph

A cumulative percentage graph permits the estimation of the percentile rank of a score and the score corresponding to a percentile rank by drawing right angled lines that intercept the curve.   For example, a score of 30 yields a percentile rank of approximately 15. Vice versa, a percentile rank of 15 yields a score of 30.

Pie charts are particularly useful in showing how components of a single variable are distributed.   Recall Table 2.3, which showed the percentages of drowning that were associated with five different age groups in North Carolina.   Figure 3.4 provides a compelling visual image of the much greater drownings among the 15 to 29 age group.   A histogram could also have presented a graphic display of these data but a pie chart introduces an element of variety.

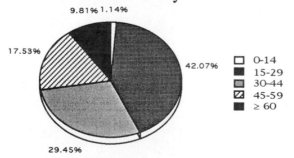

Figure 3.4   A pie chart based on Table 2.3

SELF-TEST: MULTIPLE CHOICE

1. The real limits of the score 6 are:

 a) 6.0 - 7.0   b) 5.0 - 6.0   c)   5.5 - 6.5   d) 5.9 - 6.1   e) 5.95 - 6.05

2. When we arrange a set of scores in order of magnitude and indicate the frequency associated with each score, we have constructed:

a)   a grouped frequency distribution   b) a frequency curve
c)   a histogram d) a bar graph e) a frequency distribution

3. When we collapse a scale into mutually exclusive classes and indicate the frequency associated with each class, we have constructed:

 a) a cumulative frequency distribution   b) a frequency distribution   c) a grouped frequency distribution   d) a histogram e) a nominal scale

4. Based on Table 3.3, a score of 44 has a percentile rank of approximately:

 a) 19 b) 70   c) 14 d) 90 e) 95

5. Based on Table 3.3, a percentile rank of 40 is associated with a score of approximately:

 a) 36 b) 70 c) 8 d) 14   e) none of these alternatives

6. Based on Table 3.2,   an estimate of the percentile rank of a score of 30 equals:

a) 30 b) 20 c) 55   d) 15 e) none of these alternatives

7. Based on Table 3.2,   an estimate of a score with a cumulative frequency of 14 is:

a) 40   b) 14 c) 19 d) 28   e) 20

Basing your answer on the following grouped cumulative frequency, and grouped cumulative percentage distributions, answer questions 8 through 16.

Class	f	Cumf	Cum%
35-39	2	50	100
30-34	3	48	96
25-29	7	45	90
20-24	9	38	76
15-19	14	29	58
10-14	8	15	30
5-9	5	7	14
0-4	2	2	4

8. The frequency of 3 in the class 30-34 means:

a) 3 frequencies are at the upper real limit of the class
b) 3 frequencies are at the lower real limit of the class
c) 3 frequencies are uniformly spread throughout the class
d) 3 frequencies are at the lower apparent limit of the class
e) 3 frequencies are at the upper apparent limit of the class

9. A score of 34 is slightly less than:

a) the 14th percentile b) the 58th percentile c) at the 14th percentile d) at the 7th percentile   e) none of the preceding

10. A percentile rank of 90 is slightly higher than a score of:

a) 34 b) 29 c) 24   d) 45 e) none of the preceding

11. A score of 24 is slightly less than a percentile rank of:

a) 76 b) 38 c) 20 d) 90 e) none of the preceding

12. The cumf of 29 means that 58% of the cases:

a) fall below the upper real limit of the class 15-19 b) fall above the upper real limit of the class 15-19   c) fall below the upper real limit of the class 20-24   d)   have a cumf of 15   e) insufficient information to answer

13. The percentile rank at the upper real limit (34.5) of the class 30-34 is :

a) 100   b) 48 c) 96   d) 50   e) 90

14.   The upper real limits of the classes 0-4, 5-9, and 10-14 are:

a) 4.1, 9.1, 14.1   b) 4, 9, 14 c) 4.5, 9.5, 14.5 d) 4, 9, 14.5 e) 4.5, 9, 14.5

15. The N in this sample is:

a) 100   b) 39, c) 40, d) 50 e) none of the preceding

16. The column sum that equals 50 is

a) class   b) $\Sigma f = N$ c) cumf   d) cum% e) insufficient information to answer

17. Most generally a graph may be considered:

a) a substitute for a statistical treatment of data b) a visual aid for thinking about data c) a dependable means of avoiding misinterpretation of data   d) a last resort of the uninformed e) a pictorial technique that almost always leads to misinterpretation

18. As opposed to a histogram, a bar graph is *most often used* with:

a) ratio data b) interval data c) nominal and ordinal data d) ordinal and ratio data e) nominal and interval data

19. A cumulative frequency curve of normally distributed vari-

ables will yield:

a) a J-curve b) a histogram c) a symmetrical distribution d) an ogive e) none of the preceding

The following tables show both a set of raw data and a display of EDA (exploratory data analysis). The EDA shows all the data as well as a pictorial representation that is similar to a histogram. In the top line of the EDA the three raw values shown are 12, 12, and 13.

						Cumf
12	16	24	13	1	223	3
45	27	15	32	1	567	6
17	37	28	56	2	124	9
51	22	35	46	2	5678	13
62	41	33	49	3	0234	17
52	12	25	26	3	577779	23
30	37	39	41	4	01134	28
46	53	60	44	4	5668	32
37	50	21	34	5	0123	36
37	43	57	40	5	67	38
				6	02	40

20.   The data shown in the fourth line down are:

a) 256, 257, 257, 258 b) 25, 26, 27, 28 c) 212, 214 d) 21, 22, 23   e) none of the preceding

21. The score at the 50th percentile from the EDA is estimated to be about:

a) 30   b) 35 c) 41 d) 39 e) 57

Answers: 1) c; 2) e; 3) c; 4) b; 5) b; 6) d; 7) a; 8) c; 9) e; 10) b; 11) a; 12) b; 13) c; 14) c; 15) d; 16) b 17) b; 18) c; 19) b; 20) b; 21) e

4

Measures of Central Tendency

Behavioral Objectives

1. Why is the term "average" replaced with "measures of central   tendency"?

2. Define the arithmetic mean in words as well as in algebraic form.   Calculate the mean for data sets as well as for frequency distributions.

 3. List the three properties of the mean. Identify an array of scores.

4. Distinguish between a mean and a weighed mean in words and in algebraic form.

5. Describe the median algebraically and with words. Calculate the median from an odd and even number of scores in an array.

6. Guesstimate the mean and the median by inspecting a frequency distribution.

7. Compare and contrast the mean, median, and mode in terms of their various characteristics. Explain how skewness affects the mean and the median.

Chapter Review

Central tendency is another expression for average. Statisticians prefer the term "central tendency" because of the wide use and abuse of the term "average." When you open a magazine to the latest diet fad, you may read that the average 18-year-old woman weighs 119 pounds. But what does the word average mean in this context? Is it the mean, median, or mode? Let's look at a simple example to clarify this dilemma. Shown below is an array of weight measures on a representative sample of nine 18-year-old women.

165	119	116	$\sum X = 1113$ $N = 9$
125	**119**	115	$\overline{X} = 1113/9 = 123.67$
120	119	115	Mdn and Mode $= 119$

The mean is the sum of all of these scores divided by N. In other words, $\overline{X} = \Sigma X/N = 1113/9 = 123.67$. It is clear that average, in this case, does not refer to the arithmetic mean.

Since there are nine cases in all, the median (which is the 50th percentile as we saw in Chapter 3) can be obtained by counting 5 cases down from the highest value or 5 up from the lowest value. Both procedures lead to the same median-- 119 pounds. Note also that the mode, which is the most frequent value, is also 119 pounds.

So, as you can see, it is not sufficient to use the word "average" because of its ambiguity. Note that the mean takes into account all values of the variable. If there are any extreme values, the mean is drawn toward this extreme. The woman weighing 165 pounds draws the mean toward this extreme value. However, neither the median nor the mode is influenced by extreme values. The median is the value above and below which 50% of the cases fall.   If the 165-pound woman really weighed 200 pounds, the mean would be higher but the median would remain the same as would the mode.

Now let's look at the calculation of the mean, median, and mode from a frequency distribution.

Score	f	fX	
74	2	148	
73	3	219	$\overline{X} = \Sigma fX / N$
72	7	504	
71	12	852	$= 2832 / 40$
70	8	560	
69	5	345	$= 70.80$
68	3	204	
	$N = 40$	$\Sigma fX = 2832$	

We find that the mean of the frequency distribution is 70.80.   If we had noticed that the distribution is fairly symmetrical, we could have made an accurate guess that the mean is approximately 71. By making such visual estimates, we can avoid serious calculating problems, such as entering incorrect values into the calculator or computer.

As you have seen, it is often desirable to construct a frequency distribution to eliminate repeating the many scores that occur when large amounts of data are involved. In the above distribution, it is easier to multiply 71 X 12 than to add together 71 twelve times.

Now let's look at the median and mode of the frequency, cumulative, and percentage distribution in the table below. One point is clear right at the beginning. A score of 71 has the greatest associated frequency. Therefore, the mode equals 71. Also, since the distribution is quite symmetrical, the median is approximately 71.

Score	f	Cumf	Cum%
74	2	40	100.0
73	3	38	95.0
72	7	35	87.5
71	12	28	70.0
70	8	16	40.0
69	5	8	20.0
68	3	3	7.5

The median is the 20th score in the distribution (40/2 = 20) within the score that has the true limits of 70.5 and 71.5. Without making any precise calculations, a good estimate is that it is a score of 71. More precisely, it is 4/12th of the distance above the lower real limit of the value 71, i.e., 70.5. Thus, 70.5 + 4/12 = 70.5 and .33 = 70.83. For most applications, the approximation (71) is sufficiently accurate.

There are times when a number of different samples are taken and you calculate the mean of each. You may need to know the combined, overall, or grand mean of all the samples. *If each is based on the same sample size, the calculations are easy: merely add the various means together to find their sum and then divide by the number of means you have.* For example, if you purchased 60 shares of each of four different common stocks and paid the following means per share —$8.00, $15.50, $19.00, and $22.00 -- the overall mean is (8 + 15.5 + 19 + 22) / 4 = 64.5 / 4 = $16.12.

However, if the sample size (number of shares) is *not* the

same for each transaction, you must use a procedure that takes into account the different Ns. In this situation, you must obtain what is called a *weighted mean*. The formula for the weighted mean is:

$$\overline{X}_w = \Sigma f\overline{X} / N$$

where $\Sigma f = N$ equals the total sum of means over all groups and $\overline{X}$ equals the mean of each group of scores. To illustrate, the following table shows our purchase of common stock at four different times and at four different prices. What is the overall mean price that we paid?

$\overline{X}$	f	$f\overline{X}$
mean price per share	number of shares purchased	product of f times $\overline{X}$
16.5	80	1320
24.0	120	2880
28.0	130	3640
40.5	200	8100
$\Sigma f = N = 530$		$\Sigma f\overline{X} = 15940$

The weighted mean equals 15940 / 530 = $30.08 (rounded)

Selected Exercises

1. In purchasing meat for a family of five, you paid the following prices for one-pound packages of ground chuck steak: $1.05, $1.55, $0.83 and $1.33. The mean cost per pound of these purchases was:

a) $1.43   b) $1.29   c) $0.99   d) $1.19 e) cannot answer because a weighted mean must be calculated.

2. Instead of purchasing one pound packages, you purchase 1 pound at $1.43 per pound,   2 pounds at $1.29 per pound, 3 pounds at $.99 per pound and 2 pounds at $1.19 per pound.

What was the rounded cost per pound of the 8-pound purchase?

a) $ 1.32 b) $1.24   c) $1.42 d) $1.14 e) insufficient information to answer,

3.   If one extreme score is added to a distribution, what will happen to the three measures of central tendency?

a) The median will be drawn toward the extreme score. b) The mean will be drawn toward the extreme score. c) The mode will be drawn toward the extreme score. d) All three will be drawn toward the extreme score   e) none will be affected by the extreme score.

4.   Given that a distribution of scores yields a mean of 40, a median of 38, and a mode of 36, if we added 12 points to each score, what would the new median be?

a) 38 b) 40   c) 50   d) 52 e) insufficient information to answer

5. Referring to Question 4, what is the new mean?

a) 40 b) 42 c) 50   d) 52 e) insufficient information to answer

6.   If 12 is subtracted rather than added, the mean is:

a) unchanged   b) increased by 12 points   c) decreased by 12 points   d) equal to the value of the mean divided by 12 and multiplied by N e) to answer, the value of the mean must be known

7. For a given distribution, the mode is 68, the median is 62, and the mean is 56. This distribution is:

a) normal b) symmetrical c) positively skewed d) negatively skewed e) leptokurtic

8.   When an odd number of scores is arranged in an array, the

median is:
a) the score with the greatest frequency   b) the middle score
c) the mean of the two middle scores d) the mean of the highest
and lowest scores   e) cannot be determined without additional
information

9.   When an even number of scores is arranged in an array, the
median is:

a) the score with the greatest frequency   b) the middle score
c) the mean of the two middle scores d)   the mean of the highest
and lowest scores   e) always equal to the mean

10. A group of 20 students obtained a mean score of 70 on a
quiz. A second group of 30 students obtained a mean of 80 on
the same quiz. The overall mean for the 50 students was:

a) 70 b) 74 c) 75 d) 76 e) 80

11. Which measure of central tendency yields the most
prosperous picture of income in the United States?

a) mean b) mode c) median d) weighted mean   e) all the same

12. The most frequently occurring score is:

a) any measure of central tendency b) mean c) median   d) mode
e) none of the above

13. If the median and the mean have equal values, you know
that:

a) the distribution is symmetrical b) the distribution is skewed
c) the distribution is normal d) the mode is at the center of the
distribution   e) the distribution is positively skewed

14. The mean, median, and mode are all measures of:

a) the midpoint of a distribution b) the most frequent score
c) percentile ranks   d) variability e) none of the above

15. When frequency distributions are symmetrical, it is possible to estimate with reasonable accuracy:

a) the mode b) the mean c) the median d) all of the preceding   e) none of the preceding

16. In a bell-shaped distribution of scores:

a) the mean, median, and mode have the same value b) the mean is usually a higher value than the median   c) the median is usually a higher value than the mean   d) the mean and median are the same but are different from the mode   e)   none of the preceding

17.   Which of the following constitutes the definition of the mean?

a)   the sum of all the scores divided by the number of scores b) the point in a distribution about which the summed deviations equal zero   c) the point in a distribution about which the squared deviations are minimal   d) all of the preceding   e) none of the preceding

Answers 1) d; 2) b; 3) b; 4) c; 5) d; 6 c; 7) c; 8) b; 9) c; 10) d; 11) a; 12) d; 13) a; 14) e; 15) d; 16) a; 17) d

5

Measures of Dispersion

Behavioral Objectives

1. Describe the purpose of measuring the dispersion or variability of scores about the measure of central tendency. State the relationship between the shape of the distribution and the meassurement of dispersion.

2. Define the crude range of a scale of scores. Explain the usefulness of the crude range.

3. Define and calculate the semi-interquartile range. Identify its shortcomings and its advantages.

4. Specify, both in words and in algebraic notation, the mean deviation and the sum of all the deviations from the mean without regard to sign. Explain the advantages and disadvantages of using the mean deviation.

5. Identify the purposes served by the standard deviation. In words and algebraic form, define the standard deviation and the variance. Explain the exact relationship between the variance and the standard deviation.

6. Use the crude range as the basis for gueststimating the mean and standard deviation of the data set.

Chapter Review

As we saw in Chapter 4, there are two aspects of data sets on which statisticians and researchers concentrate when quantitatively describing their key observations. We have already exemplified and discussed the first of these– the central value around which the scores in the array or distribution tend to cluster. In Chapter 5, we examine a second set of measurements that are used to describe the variability of scores or, stated another way, the extent to which the scores are dispersed or scattered about some central value.

The following table illustrates the means by which three of these measures are obtained: the crude range, the mean deviation, and two different approaches to the calculation of the *sum of squares* (SS). The sum of squares is most important since it is basic to calculating the two most important measures of dispersion.

X	$(|X - \bar{X}|)$	$(X - \bar{X})^2$	X^2
3	| 2 |	4	9
4	| 1 |	1	16
6	| 1 |	1	36
7	| 2 |	4	49

$\sum X = 20$ $\sum(|X - \bar{X}| = 6$ $\sum(X - \bar{X})^2 = 10$ $\sum X^2 = 110$

$\bar{X} = 20/4$

$\quad = 5$ $N = 4$ $MD = \sum(|X - \bar{X}|)/N = 6/4 = 1.5$

To summarize, the range is $7 - 3 = 4$; the mean deviation equals 1.5; and the sum of squares, mean deviation method, equals 10. The most frequently used method uses the raw score formula. It is used because the data sets frequently contain numerous values, and subtracting the mean from each and squaring is time consuming and likely to lead to error.

Using the raw score method, the sum of squares equals:

$$SS = \sum X^2 - (\sum X)^2 / N = 110 - (400/4) = 110 - 100 = 10$$

Note that both the mean deviation and the raw score methods yield precisely the same sum of squares, namely, 10. Incidentally, the sum of squares is a most important statistical calcualtion and will apprear again and again throughout this course.

The two measures of dispersion— the variance (s^2) and the standard deviation (s)— are easily calculated from the sum of squares.

$$s^2 = SS/N = 10/4 = 2.5$$

$$s = \sqrt{SS/N} \text{ or } \sqrt{s^2} = \sqrt{2.5} = 1.58$$

Stated verbally, the variance is the sum of the squared deviations from the mean (the sum of squares or SS) divided by

N. The standard deviation is closely related to the variance, In fact, once you have calculated the variance of a data set, you need do no more than take the square root of the variance to obtain the standard deviation.

Since the calculations of the sum of squares, the variance, and the standard deviation are the most important in the field of statistics, the following demonstrates the step by step procedures.

Score X	Score Squared X^2
39	1521
31	961
30	900
26	696
25	625
23	529

$$\Sigma X = 174 \qquad \Sigma X^2 = 5232$$

Step 1: Sum the values of the variable to obtain $\Sigma X = 174$ and count $N = 6$.

Step 2: Square each value of the variable and then sum these squared values. Thus, $\Sigma X^2 = 5232$.

Step 3: Calculate the sum of squares:
$$\begin{aligned} SS &= \Sigma X^2 - (\Sigma X)^2 / N \\ &= 5232 - (174)^2 / 6 \\ &= 5232 - 5046 \\ &= 186 \end{aligned}$$

Step 4: Find the sample variance by dividing SS by N: $s^2 = 186/6 = 31$.

Step 5:   Find the sample standard deviation by extracting the square root of the variance: $\sqrt{31}$ = 5.57.

There are a number of helpful calculations we can make if we know the mean and standard deviation of a data set that is drawn from a population that is normal or near normal.

First of all, we can ascertain how far a raw score is from the mean when expressed in terms of standard deviation units. The process of dividing the deviations of scores from the mean by the standard deviation is known as the transformation to z-scores or the z-score transformation. To illustrate, the deviation of a score of 59 from a mean of 52 is 7. If the standard deviation is 3.5, the z-score equals 7 ÷ 3.5 = 2. In other words, the raw score of 59 is two standard deviations above the mean. In equation form,

$$z = (X - \overline{X}) / s$$

As you might have observed, a raw score that is less than the mean yields a negative z-score. However, a score that is greater than the mean yields a positive z-score. Finally, a score that equals the mean results in a z-score that is equal to zero. For practice, find the z-scores of the following values of the variable —10, 12, 21— when the mean equals 12 and the standard deviations equals 5. The answers, respectively, are: -.40, 0, and 1.80.

One of the advantages of transforming raw scores to z-scores for normally distributed variables is that it enables us to compare an individual's performance on two or more unrelated tasks. Suppose we wanted to compare an astronaut's score on a manual dexterity test with her comprehension on an abstract verbal task. If we knew only that she score 20 on the dexterity task and 540 on the verbal task, we could say little about her comparitive performance on each task. But suppose we knew that the mean and standard deviations of scores on the dexterity task is 18 and 2, respectively. Her z-score on manual dexterity would be z = (20 - 18) / 2 = 1.00. Thus, relative to the mean, her score is one standard deviation above the mean. Suppose next that the mean and standard deviation on the abstract verbal task are 500 and 20 respectively. Her z-score would be (540 - 500) / 20 = 2.00. Since both z-scores are positive, we know that she scored higher than the mean on both tasks, Moreover, since her z-score on the verbal task (z = 2.00) is higher than her z-score on the dexterity task (z = 1.00), we know that she performed higher on the verbal test than she did on the dexterity task.

If the tasks are normally distributed, the standard normal distribution may be used to chararacterize more precisely each z-score. When plotted on a graph, any normal distribution is symmetrical and bell-shaped. In the standard normal distribution, the mean is equal to zero and the standard deviation equals 1.00. Moreover, the total area under the curve is 1.00, making it easy to express area above and below various z-scores as total areas. By multiplying these proportions by 100, we can express these areas as percentages of total area under the curve.

SELF-TEST: MULTIPLE CHOICE

1. Of all the measures of dispersion, which is the least stable?

a) the semi-interquartile range   b) the standard deviation   c) the mean deviation   d) the crude range   e) none of the preceding

2. The standard deviation is the square root of:

a) the crude range   b) the variance   c) the semi-interquartile range   d) the mean deviation   e) the arithmetic mean

3. Which statistic does not belong to the others in the group?

a) range   b) mean   c) semi-interquartile range   d) standard deviation   e) mean deviation

4. $(\sum X)^2$ is equal to:

a) $\sum X^2$ b) the sum of the square of each value of X   c) NX^2
d) all of the preceding   e) none of the preceding

5. Which grouping of scores exhibits the least variability?

a) 2, 4, 6, 8, 10, 12   b) 2, 3, 4, 10, 11, 12   c) 2, 6, 7, 7, 8, 12
d) 2, 2, 3, 11, 12, 12   e) the variability is all the same

6. Which grouping of scores exhibits the most variability?

a) 2, 4, 6, 8, 10, 12   b) 2, 3, 4, 10, 11, 12   c) 2, 6, 7, 7, 8, 12
d) 2, 2, 3, 11, 12, 12   e) the variability is all the same

7. Reducing the frequency in the middle of a distribution will:

a)   increase the standard deviation   b) reduce the standard deviation c) not affect the standard deviation d) depend on the N
e)   depend on the range

8 . Reducing the frequency of scores at the tails of a distribution:
a)   increases the standard deviation   b) reduces the standard
deviation c) does not affect the standard deviation d) depends
on the N   e)   depends on the range

9.   Which of the following measures of variability is not dependent on the precise value of all the scores?

a) range b) mean deviation c) standard deviation d) variance
e) none of the preceding

10. In a frequency distribution with a mean of 50 and a standard
deviation of 10, six scores of 10 are added to the distribution.
The recomputed value of the standard deviation will be:

a) greater than the original s b) less than the original s c) unchanged d) dependent on the N in the original group   e) 60%
of the original s

Questions 11 through 14 refer to the following information: The
mean score of 500 students on a statistics exam is 45 with s = 5.

11. If two points were *added* to each of the 500 scores, the new s
would be:

a) 2.5 b) 3 c) 5 d) 5 ÷ (2/500) e) 7

12. If two points were *subtracted* from each of the 500 scores,
the new s would be:

a) 2.5 b) 3 c) 5 d) 5 ÷ (2/500) e) 7

13) If each score were doubled, the new s would be:

a) 2.5 b) 5 c) 7 d) 10 e) 5 + (2/500)

14) If each score were divided in half, the new s would be:

a) 2.5 b) 5 c) 7 d) 10 e) 5 + (2/500)

15) The mean score of 30 students on an exam is 47 and the standard deviation is 0. The distribution of scores:

a) is mesokurtic   b) is normal   c) contains many negative scores   d) shows all students scored 47   e) contains insufficient information

16. Each of the following frequency distributions has the same top and bottom scores. Which one has the largest standard deviation?

a) a U distribution   b) a positively skewed distribution c) a normal distribution   d) a negatively skewed distribution e) an abnormal distribution

17. Which of the following measures is generally our most useful indicator of dispersion?

a) the range   b) the semi-interquartile range c) the standard deviation   d) the mean deviation   e) all are about equally useful

18.   Which measure of dispersion reflects only the two most extreme scores in a distribution?

a) the mean deviation   b) the standard deviation   c) the range d) the semi-interquartile range e) the variance

19. Which measure of dispersion is defined as the sum of the deviations from the mean divided by N?

a) the range   b) the variance c) the mean deviation   d) the standard deviation (e) no measure of dispersion is so defined

20. The mean of a normal distribution of scores is 100 and s = 10. The percentage of area between 100 and 110 is:

a) 68 b) 84 c) 50 d) 34 e) 16

21. The mean of a normal distribution of scores is 100 and s = 10. The percentage of area between 90 and 110 is:

a) 68 b) 84 c) 50 d) 34 e) 16

22. Which z-score corresponds to the 44th percentile?

a) -1.56 b) -0.44 c) 0.15 d) -0.15   e) 1.56

23. Which z-score corresponds to the 99th percentile?

a) 0.99 b) 0 .49 c) 2.33 d) 2.00   e) 0 .01

24.   Assume: an individual obtains a score of 94, the population mean is estimated at 100, and the population standard deviation equals 3. The person's z-score is equal to:

a) 2.00 b) 3.00 c) 4.00   d) -4.00   e) -2.00

Questions 25 through 27 refer to a normal distribution with a mean of 100 and a standard deviation of 15:

25. A score of 120 has a percentile rank of:

a) 9 b) 41 c) 59 d) 82 e) 91

26. The z-score at the 75th percentile is:

a) 90 b) 110 c)   123 d)   127 e) between 115 and 125

27.   The percentage of people with scores between 75 and 85 is

the same as the percentage of those who have scores between:

a) 90 and 100   b) 95 and 105   c) 110 and 120   d) 115 and 125
e)   none of the preceding

ANSWERS   1) d;   2) b;   3) b;   4) e;   5) c;   6) d;   7) a;
8) b;   9) a;   10) a;   11) c;   12) c;   13) d;   14) a;   15) d;
16) a;   17) c;   18) c;   19) e;   20) d;   21) a;   22) d;   23) c;
24) e;   25) e;   26) b;   27) d

6

Correlation

Behavioral Objectives

1. Define the functions served by correlational coefficients. State the three factors that influence the appropriate correlation to use.

2. State the characteristics that are common to all correlation coefficients

3. Define Pearson r in words and in algebraic notation. Describe the relationship between Pearson r and z-scores. Specify when Pearson r is appropriate for describing the relationship between two variables.

4. Identify the formula for the raw score method of calculating Pearson r.

5. State some alternative possibilities for explaining low correlations when Pearson r is used to quantify the extent of the relationship between two variables. Explain how a truncated range might affect the size of the correlation coefficient.

6. Describe when the Spearman r_s is appropriate for ascertaining the correlation between two variables. Define Spearman r_s in words and in algebraic form.

Chapter Review

Scientists routinely examine countless hypotheses in which the relation between and among two or more variables are of crucial importance. Consider the following: What is the relation, if any, among disease, dietary cholesterol, depression, smoking, dietary fiber, vitamin deficiency, and regular exercise? What about those who smoke a pack a day or more? Are they at risk for circulatory and respiratory disorders?

In raising questions of this sort, we are concerned with the relation among two or more variables. To express quantitatively the extent to which two variables are related (i.e., vary together or *covary*), we calculate a statistic known as a *correlation coefficient.*

Our first correlation coefficient is the Pearson r.   The Pearson r is used with interval/ratio scaled data. Although appropriate for many types of such data, there are instances in which the Pearson r is not appropriate— namely when the graph of the relationships between the two variables does not approach a straight line.   It is said to be nonlinear or even curvilinear. Both types of relations are shown in Figure 6.1

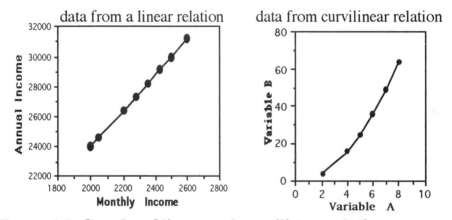

Figure 6.1 Graphs of linear and curvilinear relations

As with the variance and standard deviation in Chapter 5, the calculation of SS (Sum of Squares) is of critical importance. The denominator of the raw score formula for the Pearson r involves calculating the sum of squares of each variable, multiplying them together, and taking the square root of their product. Even the numerator is analogous to the sum of squares of the two variables. In the first term, you multiply each value of X by its corresponding Y and sum these values, i.e., ΣXY. The second term requires the sum of the X and Y values, multiplying these sums together $[(\Sigma X) \cdot (\Sigma Y)]$ and dividing by N.

The simplest formula, then, is:

$$r = \frac{\Sigma XY \ - \ (\Sigma X)(\Sigma Y) / \ N}{\sqrt{SS_X \cdot \ SS_Y}}$$

Recall that $SS_X = [\Sigma X^2 - (\Sigma X)^2]/N$ and $SS_Y = [\Sigma Y^2 - (\Sigma Y^2)]/N$. In other words, the calculation of Pearson r adds very little in the way of computation than the calculations performs in the preceding chapter.

X	Y	X^2	Y^2	$X \cdot Y$
83.0	87.0	6889	7569	7221
72.0	79.0	5184	6241	5688
67.0	74.0	4489	5476	4958
58.0	63.0	3364	3969	3654
77.0	76.0	5929	5776	5852
62.0	80.0	3844	6400	4960
95.0	91.0	9025	8281	8645
80.0	89.0	6400	7921	7120
71.0	77.0	5041	5929	5467
Sum 665	716	50165	57562	53565

$$SS_X = 50165 - (665)^2/9 = 50165 - 49136,11 = 1028.89$$

$$SS_Y = 57562 - (716)^2/9 = 57562 - 516961.78 = 600.22$$

$$\Sigma XY - (\Sigma X)(\Sigma Y)/N = 53565 - (665)(716)/9 = 660.56$$

$$r = 600,56 / \sqrt{1028.89 \times 600.22} = 660.56/785.86 = .84$$

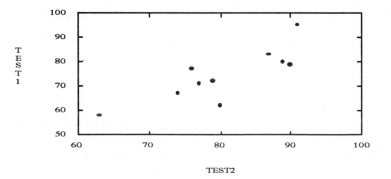

TEST2

As you can see, the correlation is quite high -- 0.84. Note also that the nine pairs of scores extend from the lower left hand corner (low values in each member of a pair) to the upper right hand corner (high values in each member of a pair). Indeed, the correlation is quite high. Individuals scoring high on X also score relatively high on Y and those scoring low on X score fairly low on Y.

When one variable is measured on an ordinal scale and the other is ordinal or higher, the Spearman r or r_s is the measure of choice. Spearman r is often referred to as the rank correlation coefficient because both variables must be expressed as ranks prior to calculating r_s. This is the case even if the scale of one of the variables is interval or ratio.

The formula to use in calculating Spearman r is:

$$r_s = 1 - \frac{6 \Sigma D^2}{N(N^2 - 1)}$$

In the table below, the X-variable consists of subjective evaluations of a supervisor or the on-job performance of eight employees. Scores were based on the number of performance errors assigned by the supervisor. The higher the numerical value assigned by the supervisor to an employee, the poorer was the evaluation of the performance assigned to that employee. The variable is assumed to be ordinal since the score units cannot be assumed to be interval/ratio. The errors were not all equal blunders. The Y-variable is the number of days late to work (20 minutes or more) during a six month period. Thus, the Y-variable is a discrete ratio variable in which the number of days late are counted and considered equal in performance. Since the Y-variable is ordinal, both variables should be rank ordered from least serious error to the greatest error in performance. The following table shows both the ranking procedures and the use of these rankings in Spearman's r. Notice that, when two ranks are tied scores (12 in the Y- variable), they share ranks of 4 and 5 and so the both are assigned the mean of the rank (4.5). The next rank is 6. If there are three tied ranks, such as ties for ranks 6, 7, and 8, all three are assigned the middle rank (7) and the next value is assigned a rank of 9. Note that the sum of the differences is equal to zero. If not, an error has been made either in assigning ranks or in subtracting Y-ranks from X-ranks.

Employee	X	Y	Rank of X	Rank of Y	Difference	D^2
1	30	12	4	4.5	-0.5	0.25
2	24	16	2	8	-6	36
3	42	10	7	3	4	16
4	39	8	5	2	3	9
5	45	14	8	7	1	1
6	40	7	6	1	5	25
7	20	13	1	6	-5	25
8	28	12	3	4.5	-1.5	2.25
				Sum	0	114.5

$$\text{Spearman } r = 1 - \frac{6(114.5)}{8 \times 63} = 1 - \frac{687}{540}$$

$$= 1 - 1.27 = -0.27$$

As we can see, there appears to be a small negative correlation between supervisory evaluation and lateness performance. In other words, if you were frequently late, you might obtain a somewhat better evaluation than if you were regularly on time. In inferential statistics, we would raise the question as to whether this sample correlation and the sample N were sufficiently high to rule it out as a chance occurrence. This can be seen on the scatter diagram on page 65.

SELF-TEST: MULTIPLE CHOICE

1. If you get a product moment correlation coefficient of 0.50, then the rank correlation coefficient will be approximately:

a) 0; b) .25; c) .50; d) 1.0   e) there is no way to estimate the answer

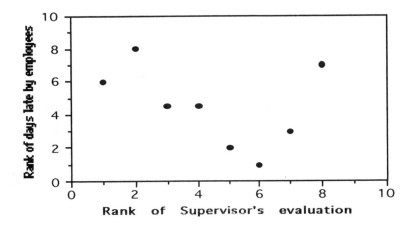

2.   A correlation between college entrance exam grades and scholastic achievement was found to be - 1.08. On the basis of this finding, you would tell the university that:

a) the entrance exam is a good predictor of success   b) they should hire a new statistician c) the exam is a good test   d) students who do best on this exam will become the worst students e) students at this school are underachieving

3. It is possible to compute a coefficient of correlation if you are given:

a) one score   b)   two measurements on the same individual   c) 50 scores on a clerical aptitude test   d) all of the preceding   e) none of the preceding

4.   You have correlated speed of different cars with gasoline mileage and found r = 0.35.   You later discovered that all speedometers were set 5 miles per hour too fast. You recompute r, using corrected scores. What will the new r be?

a) -0.30 b) 0.40   c) 0.30 d) -0.35 e) 0.35

5.   You have correlated height in feet with weight in ounces. You found that r = 0.65. You decided to recompute after you transformed the height in feet into inches. What will the new r

be?

a) 0.05 b) 0.40 c) -0.07 d) 0.65 e) 0.48

6. Truncated range:

a) increases r   b) decreases r   c) does not affect r   d) is a concept that does not affect r   e) none of the preceding

7. The correlation between midterm and final grades for 300 students is 0.62. If 5 points are added to each midterm grade, the new r will be:

a) 0 .12 b) 0.57 c) 0.62   d) 0.67 e) 0.74

8. After several studies,   Professor Smith concludes that there is a zero correlation between body weight and bad temper. This means that:

a) heavy people tend to have bad tempers   b) skinny people have bad tempers c) no one has a bad temper   d) everyone has a bad temper e) people with a bad temper tend to span the weight spectrum

9. Which of the following representations concerning Pearson r is *not true?*

a) r = 0.00 represents the absence of a linear relationship   b) for Pearson r to be a valid statistic the relationship between the two variables must be nonlinear   c) r = 0.76 has the same predictive power as r = -0.76   d) r = 1.00 is a perfect linear relationship e) all of the above are true statements

10. The correlation between I.Q. and grade performance was found to be 0.64 for 8000 students at State U. When the same study was conducted for 2000 students in the honors program, the obtained coefficient was 0.16. Which of the following might explain the difference between the two studies?

a) There were one quarter as many students in the second study.
b) The students in the honors program represent a more

homogeneous group; thus, the problem was truncated range. c) The majority of students in the university are not as intelligent as those in the honors program.   d) The relationship between I.Q. and grade performance is curvilinear for the second group. e) The statistician made an   error.

11.   When the relationship between the two variables is curvilinear, the Pearson r will be:

a) 0.00 b) negative c) positive   d) some value between -0.50 and -0.20   e) Pearson r will not be appropriate

12. Two variables, X and Y, are to be correlated. The mean of the distribution of the X variable and the standard deviation equals 0. The Pearson r will be:

a) 0.00 b) 0.50 c) -0.50   d) 1.00   e) -1.00

13. The correlation coefficient obtained from identical values of a single pair of measurements is:

a) 0.00 b) 0.50 c) -0.50   d) 1.00   e) impossible to calculate

14.   The correlation coefficient obtained with two pairs of measurements (assuming no tied score for either variable) will be:

a) either 0.00 or 1.00   b) either 0.00 or -1.00   c)   between 1.00 or - 1.00 d) either 0.50 or -0.50 e) impossible to calculate

15.   Decreasing the range between two variables often causes the correlation between the two variables to:

a) decrease   b) increase c) remain the same d) vary randomly e) there is no way to know the answer

16.   Which of the following assumptions is required for *interpreting* Pearson r?

a) linearity   b) homoscedasticity b) normality d) all of the preceding   e) none of the preceding

17. Which of the following statements is true for the Pearson r but not for the Spearman r?

a) A positive r means that a person scoring low in one variable is likely to score low on the second variable. b) Two sets of measurements must be obtained on the same individuals (or events) or on pairs of individuals (or events). c) The value of r must be between and including +1.00 and -1.00. d) If an individual scores substantially low on the X variable he or she will probably score low on the second variable for each correlational measure. e) All of the preceding apply to both correlational coefficients.

18.   The Spearman r should be the correlation coefficient of choice when:

a) one measure is interval and the other measure is ratio   b) at least one measure is ordinal   c) both measures are interval   d) both measures are ordinal   e) both measures are ratio

19.   Of the values obtained on two variables:

a) only one variable is displayed in a scatter diagram   b) the number of variables displayed in a scatter diagram is a matter of choice c) variables are displayed in a scatter diagram   d) all of the preceding e) none of the preceding.

20.   In the event of tied scores when ranking a variable in preparation for calculating Spearman r:

a) assign the mean rank of the tied scores b) assign the ranks at random   c)   discard the tied values   d) ignore the ties   e) none of the preceding

ANSWERS   1) c; 2) b; 3) e; 4) e; 5) d; 6) b; 7) c;   8) e; 9) b; 10) b; 11) e; 12) a; 13) e; 14) c; 15) a; 16) d; 17) e; 18, b; 19) c; 20) e

7

An Introduction to Regression and Prediction

Behavioral Objectives

1. Given that Pearson r equals either +1, 0, or -1, specify the best way to predict the value of one variable from knowledge of another variable.

2. Define the regression line and explain what is meant by "best fit." Specify the formulas for obtaining the slope of the regression line of Y on X or of X on Y, using the value of Pearson r and the standard deviations of X and Y.

3. Describe the similarities between the regression line and the mean. Explain the procedures for constructing lines of regression. State the relationship between the X and Y regression lines and the magnitude of r.

4. Define the term "residual variance" in words and in algebraic notation. Similarly, define the standard error of estimate in words as well as algebraic notation. Describe what happens to the standard error of estimate as the magnitude of r increases. Compare how changes in the magnitude of r affect the explained and unexplained variation.

5. Define and distinguish among the variations of scores around the sample mean and such concepts as unexplained variance and explained variance, State the relationship among total variation, explained variation, and unexplained variation.

6. Describe the relationship between correlation and causation.

Chapter Review

Think for a moment of the number of times in a day that we use past experience as the basis for anticipating future outcomes. When we study hard, long, and diligently in preparation for an exam, we expect to do well. When we go to our fa-vorite restaurant or fast food joint, we expect to achieve gusta-tory satisfaction.

Of course, the majority of predictions we make in every-day life are subjective, informal, and not often accompanied with reams of data. However, the processes of prediction in real life do not differ greatly from the processes involved in statistical pre-diction. Both involve an estimate of past or present records and both require that we make an effort to assess the de-pendability of these records or data as guides to other sets of data.

In Chapter 6, we examined correlation as a means of determining the extent to which two variables are related. Pre-sumably, the higher the correlation between two variables the better we are able to predict values of one variable from knowledge of another variable.

In Chapter 7 we examined a straight line fitted to the scatter diagram: we called this a line of regression. There are, in fact, two lines of regression for one set of correlated data: the regression of Y on X (i.e., predicting Y-values from X-values) and the line of regression of X on Y (i.e., predicting X-values from Y-values). We covered only the first of these in the text although the second procedure is essentially the same.

Let's start out by looking at two sample sets of data. The correlation is +1.00 in the first and -1.00 in the second. In other words, the correlation is perfect in both cases.

Variables	Set 1 Correlation is +1.00		Set 2 Correlation is -1.00	
	X	Y	X	Y
	1	1	1	4
	2	2	2	3
	3	3	3	2
	4	4	4	1

The figures below show the scatter diagram of both sets with the line of regression imposed on both scatter diagrams.

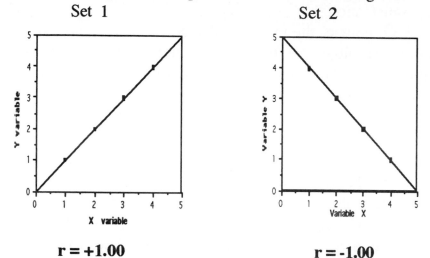

Set 1

Set 2

r = +1.00

r = -1.00

As is immediately visible, when the correlation is either perfect positive or perfect negative, the regression line runs through each of the X and Y data points. Note, in the graph of r = +1.00, our prediction of Y from each value of X is accurate. Thus, if X = 1.00 Y = 1.00. If X = 4, Y = 4. The same applies for predicting Y from X when r = -1.00. If X = 4, Y = 1. Similarly, if X = 1, Y = 4.

In data collected in the behavioral sciences, the cor-relations are usually considerably less than ± 1.00. What happens when our correlations are *not* perfect? Our data points will not all lie on a straight line. They will be scattered about the regression line with the degree of scatter depending on the magnitude of the correlation. If the correlation is very high, most of the points representing the paired values of the two variables will lie close to the line. If the correlation is low, the data points will be more widely scattered about the regression line. If the correlation is 0.00, the slope will zero, the Y-intercept of this line will be the mean of Y, and all points on the regression line will equal the mean of Y for all values of X.

When the correlation is less than perfect, there exists no straight line that contains all of the points. What we must find is the straight line that best fits the data. The best fitting line is the

regression line.
        The regression line, or line of "best fit," is defined as the straight line that makes the squared deviations around it minimal. The deviations referred to are the distances from the points in the scatter diagram to the line of best fit. Let us look at a data set and the superimposed regression line when the correlation is greater than zero. In the following table we see the scores of 10 students on a math proficiency test and quality point average. The correlation between the two variables is shown as well as the standard deviation of both variables.

| Math Test | QPA | | | |
X	Y	X squared	Y squared	X times Y
45	2	2025	4	90
40	2.5	1600	6.25	100
35	2	1225	4	70
30	1.5	900	2.25	45
30	1	900	1	30
30	1	900	1	30
20	0.5	400	0.25	10
20	0.5	400	0.25	10
10	0.5	1000	.25	5
260	11.5	8450	19.25	390

$N = 9$ X Sum of squares = 938.89   Y sum of squares = 4.56

Sum XY = 57.78 $r = 57.78/ \sqrt{(938.89)(4.56)} = 0.88$
$\overline{X} = 260/9 = 28.889$ $\overline{Y} = 11.5/9 = 1.278$

Standard deviation of X = 10.21   Standard deviation of Y = 0.71

_____

        You may note that, even though the correlation between the two variables is quite high (r = .88), the regression line does not pass through all the data points. Nevertheless, the distance between the data points and the regression is observably less than their distance from the Y-mean,
        To draw the regression line, you need only use the formula for predicting two Y-values (Y') from X-values at both

Figure 7.1   The regression line for predicting Y from X superimposed over the scatter diagram of two correlated variables

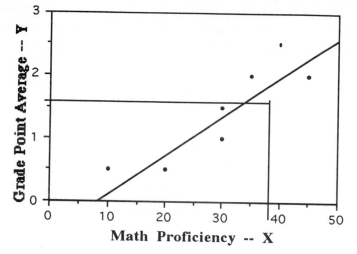

ends of the X-distribution and then draw a straight line joining these two predicted values (Figure 7.1)..

Let us briefly review the terminology of prediction. The symbol Y', usually pronounced "Y prime" or "Y predicted," is the predicted value of Y from values of X. The formula for predicting Y' from values of X is:

$$Y' = \overline{Y} + r \frac{s_Y}{s_X} (X - \overline{X})$$

Thus, if you wanted to predict Y' from X = 38, the answer would be:

$$
\begin{aligned}
Y' &= 1.278 + .88\,(.71/10.21)(38 - 28.88) \\
&= 1.278 + (.0612)(9.11) \\
&= 1.278 + .558 \\
&= 1.84
\end{aligned}
$$

You can also look at the above scattergram and construct a right-angled line until it intercepts the regression line. You can then read directly to the left vertical line and you will find that you have a good approximation to a predicted Y-value of 1.84.

The regression line is a sort of moving mean and shares some of the characteristics of the mean. Let's expand on the similarity of mean for single-variable distributions with the regression line for two variable (bivariate) distributions. Just as you can calculate a standard deviation from the mean based on the deviations of values of the variable from the mean, so also can you calculate a standard deviation from bivariate distributions based on the deviations of scores from the regression line. This standard deviation is called the standard error of estimate. Just as the standard deviation indicates how widely dispersed the scores are about its mean, the standard error of estimate gives us an idea as to how widely dispersed the scores are about the regression line. There are two standard estimates for bivariate distributions, one around the regression line for predicting Y-values from X-values and the other involved with the regression line for predicting X-values from values of Y.   We'll look only at the standard error of estimate for predicting Y from X.

The following is the formula for computing the estimate around the regression line of Y on X.

$$s_{esty} = s_y \sqrt{1 - r^2}$$

Using the math proficiency test example, $s_{esty} = .780 \sqrt{.19} = 0.34$.

SELF-TEST: MULTIPLE CHOICE

Questions 1 through 9 refer to the following statistics:

$$\overline{X} = 35 \qquad\qquad \overline{Y} = 50$$
$$s_x = 5 \qquad\qquad s_y = 10$$

1. If r = 0, what is the best prediction on the Y-variable for X = 45?

a) 30   b) 40   c) 50   d) 60   e) insufficient information to answer

2. If r = 0.50, what is the best prediction on the Y-variable for X

= 45?

a) 30   b) 40   c) 50   d) 60   e) insufficient information to answer

3. If r = -0.50, what is the best prediction on the Y-variable for X = 45?

a) 30 b) 40 c) 50 d) 60 e) 70

4. If r = +1.00, what is the best prediction on the Y-variable for X = 45?

a) 30 b) 40 c) 50 d) 60 e) 70

5. If r = -1.00, what is the best prediction on the Y variable for X = 45?

a) 30 b) 40 c) 50 d) 60 e) 70

6. If r = 0.50, what is the best prediction on the Y-variable for X = 35?

a) 48 b) 49 c) 50 d) 51 e) 52

7. If r = -0.50, what is the best prediction on the Y-variable for X = 35?

a) 48 b) 49 c) 50 d) 51 e) 52

8. If r = 1.00, what is the best prediction on the Y-variable for X = 35?

a) 48 b) 49 c) 50 d) 51 e) 52

9. The standard estimate of Y equals:

a) 0.16 b) 0.07 c) 5.72 d) 10.53 e) none of the preceding

10. The equation Y = -X is an example of:

a) a negative correlation b) a straight line c) neither a nor b   d) both a and b e)   a zero correlation

11. If a person scored 2 standard deviations below the mean on one variable, our best guess is that he or she:

a) scored 2 standard deviations below the mean on a correlated variable   b) scored 2 standard deviations above the mean on an uncorrelated second variable c)   scored 0 standard deviations above and below the mean on a second variable d) insufficient information to make an informed guess e) none of the preceding

12. The explained variation is defined as:

a) the sum of squares of the deviations of scores around the sample mean b) the sum of squares of the deviations of scores around the regression line   c) the sum of squares of the predicted scores around the sample mean   d) the coefficient of determination e) none of the preceding

13.   In the event of a perfect correlation, there is :

a) no unexplained variation   b) no total variation   c)   no explained variation   d) no coefficient of determination   d) all of the preceding are valid statements

14.   If r = 0.49, the coefficient of determination is :

a) 0.70 b) 0 .24 c) 0.98 d) 0.49 e) none of the preceding

15.   If there is a high negative correlation:

a) unexplained variation is high b) total variation is low c) explained variation is low d) explained variation is high   e) explained variation equals unexplained variation

16. If the correlation between body weight and income is high and positive, we could conclude that:

a) high incomes cause people to eat more food   b) low incomes cause people to eat less food   c) high-income people spend a greater proportion of their income on food   d) all of the above e) none of the preceding.

17. If the percentage of variation in one variable associated with another variable is 0.25, then r must be equal to:

a) 0 .50   b) 0.25   c) 0.90   d) 0.60   e) 0.625

ANSWERS   1) c; 2) d; 3) b; 4) e; 5) a; 6) c; 7) c; 8) c; 9) a; 10) c; 11) d; 12) b; 13) a; 14) b; 15) d; 16) e; 17) a

8

Probability

Behavioral Objectives

1. Know the role of probability theory in inferential statistics. Is probability central or peripheral to the making of inferences?
2. Know the three different approaches to probability, the characteristics of each, and when each approach is appropriate.
3. Know the limits within which the values of probabilities must fall. Show the various ways in which probability may be expressed.
4. Define the addition rule and know under what circumstances it is applied. Know when to apply the addition rule when events are *not* mutually exclusive and when they *are* mutually exclusive.
5. Define the multiplication rule. Learn when to apply the multiplication rule in different situations. Distinguish between independent and dependent occurrences.
6. Distinguish between sampling with and without replacement. Know the circumstances under which these two methods of sampling may yield large differences in probability values.
7. Know the formula for obtaining probability values of continuous rather than discrete variables. Be able to relate z-scores to probability.

Chapter Review

With this chapter, we entered a new realm of statistics, that of inferential statistics. All the topics we have covered thus far —percentiles, central tendency, dispersion, correlation, and prediction— are considered under the heading of descriptive statistics. The measures of descriptive statistics help us to picture and quantify a data set, conceptually and visually, and to organize and summarize the data in convenient and usable form. The methods of inferential statistics take us one step further. With inferential statistics, we shall learn how to generalize our conclusions from samples of data to the populations from which they were taken. For example, suppose we chose a sample of randomly selected students from a school district in Milwaukee in order to test certain measures under consideration for adoption.   The techniques of inferential statistics will permit us to generalize our finding from our sample to the large population under consideration.

In this process of generalization, we will use descriptive statistical measures with which you are already familiar, such as the mean , the sum of squares, and the standard deviation based on the sum of squares.   We begin our discussion with the basics of probability.   You should not take this chapter lightly, for it includes concepts to which you will return time and again while learning the basic principles of statistical inference.

The first concept is that of randomness.   When we are interested in drawing inferences about populations from samples, we want the sample to be representative of the population in which we are interested.   This is one aspect of randomness.   The other — random assignment to experimental conditions —permits us to avoid various biases from infiltrating these conditions.

Probability theory is concerned with the possible outcomes of experiments.   If a scientist is studying fluctuations in weight, there are three possible outcomes for each member in the sample: weight gain, no negligible change, and weight loss.

Within probability, there are three approaches to assigning probability values to outcomes and events: classical, empirical, and subjective.   In the classical approach, relative frequencies are assigned according to theory.   The assumption of a classical approach is that an ideal situation exists in which all of the possible outcomes are known or describable.   Although we can construct situations in which all of the population members can be counted and their associated probabilities calculated through reasoning rather than experience, it is not always possible to do so.   However, let us consider an instance in which knowing all possible outcomes permits us to apply the classical approach to probability.

Consider the toss of a single hypothetical die in which there are a limited number of outcomes— six. Assuming that each event has an equal likelihood of occurring, we can calculate the probability of obtaining any given outcome by using the probability formula:

$$p(A) = \frac{\text{number of outcomes favoring event A}}{\text{total number of possible events}}$$

Suppose we are interested in determining the probability that we shall obtain a 5 on a single toss of a die. Knowing there is only one outcome favoring this event and there are six possible outcomes, we can determine that $p(5) = 1/6$.

In the behavioral sciences we do not often know all possible outcomes or the exact probability that is associated with any single outcome. We must estimate these probabilities on the basis of past observations of samples taken at random from the population. The basic distinction between the empirical and the classical approaches is the method of assigning relative frequencies to each of the possible outcomes. With the classical approach, this is accomplished through the assumption of an ideal situation in which the frequencies of the outcomes are known or may be calculated. The many gambling casinos in Las Vegas, Atlantic City, and Monaco make fortunes through knowing probabilities associated with the rolls of dice and the dealing of playing cards. Their gains are augmented by discarding these tools of profit after a few hours of use before the corners of the dice or the cards show wear. Thoughtful players may observe these biases and play them to the disadvantage of the house.

In the empirical   approach, relative frequencies are determined through observation.   What is the proportion of genuinely red-haired people in the population? This can be known only through careful observation. Then there are subjective probabilities that are based more on hunches or intuition. No matter how the probability of the single event is obtained, whether by the classical, empirical, or subjective approach, the rules for adding and multiplying probabilities remain the same.

Using our example of the die, suppose we are interested in obtaining an even number (2, 4, or 6) *on a single trial*. We solve this problem by use of the addition rule of mutually exclusive events: the pobability of obtaining one of a set of mutually exclusive events is equal to the sum of the separate probabilities of each of these events, In symbolic notation, p(2 or 4 or 6) = p(2) + p(4) + p(6) = 1/6 + 1/6 + 1/6 = 3/6 or 1/2

What do you suppose your chances are of obtaining an even number on *two successive tries or trials?* We must now apply the multiplication rule: the probability of the simultaneous or successive occurrence of two events is the product of the separate probabilities of each event. Restated, the multiplication rule becomes: p(A and B) = p(A)(B) in which event A is the occurrence of an even number on the first toss (p(A) = 1/2) and p(B) is the occurrence of an even number on the second toss (p(B) = 1/2).   Thus, the probability of obtaining an even number on two tosses of a single die (or a simultaneous toss of a pair of dice) is p(A)p(B) =(1/2)(1/2) = 1/4 or 0.25.

Now that we have summarized the addition and multiplication probability rules, let's consider these rules and theory of probability as they relate to continuous variables and the normal curve. For continuous variables, we define probability in a somewhat different manner.   Instead of regarding probability as a ratio of outcomes, we now define it as a ratio of areas:

$$p = \frac{\text{areas under portions of a curve}}{\text{total area under the curve}}$$

The curve to which we refer is based on the standard normal curve model,   Specifically, we will uses z-scores and the areas under the normal curve related to these scores. Recall that the total area under the standard normal curve is 1.00. The denominator in the probability formula will always be 1.00.

Using the areas under the normal curve in combination with the addition and multiplication rules, we can determine probabilities that are associated with a score occurring singly or jointly with other scores. To illustrate:

Given μ = 25 and σ = 8, what is the probability of obtaining a score of 31 or less?

$$z = \frac{31 - 25}{8} = 0.75$$

Checking in Table A in the statistical appendix of the text, you will find that 0.2266 is the area beyond a 0.75. To find the area below a z-score of 0.75, you merely subtract 0.2266 from 1.00 (the total area under the curve). You will obtain an area of 0.7734. When you set up your probability proportion, you will have:

$$p = \frac{0.7734}{1.00} = 0.7734$$

So you see, the probability of scoring 31 or lower, rounded to the second decimal place, is 0.77 or 77 chances in one hundred.

What is the probability of achieving a score at or below 31 or a score of 41 or greater? This sort of question calls for the use of the addition rule of probability. When you must find the probability of *either* of two or more events, you should find the probability of each of the single events and then apply the addition rule. Thus, $z \leq 31 = 75$, $p_{\leq 31} = .07734$; $z_{\leq 41} = 16/8 =$, $p_{\leq 41} = 0.0228$. Therefore, the probability of scoring equal to or less than 31 or equal to or greater than 41 is $.7724 + 0.0228 = 0.7962$ rounded to 80. Note that you can also find the probability of scoring between 31 and 41 is $1.00 - 0.80 = 0.20$.

SELF-TEST: MULTIPLE CHOICE

1. A p value equal to 1.00 means that the event:

a) has a low probability (1 in 100) of occurring   b) is reasonably certain to occur   c) is certain to occur   d) is reasonably certain not to occur e) has about a 50-50 chance of occurring

2. If an event has 80 chances in 100 of occurring, its associated probability is:

a) 80 b) 8.00 c) 0 .20 d) 0.08 e) 0 .80

3) If p = 0.30, the chances the event will occur are:

a) 30 in 50 b) 2 to 1 against   c) 3 out of 10   d) 3 out of 100
d) 1 in 30

4.   An investigator reporting that the mean of the experimental
group was five points higher than the control group may conclude that:

a) the experimental variable had an effect   b) the experimental
variable had only a small effect   c) the probability is 0.05 that
the experimental variable had an effect   d) the control variable
had no effect e) probability information is needed to form a
conclusion

5. If any event in a series has no predictable effect on another,
the events may be said to be:

a) independent b) correlated c) biased d) reliable e) systematic

6. Distributions of sample statistics based on large random
samples drawn from a population:

a) generally take unpredictable forms   b) are biased   c) evidence no reliable relationship to the population parameters d)
precisely duplicate the parent distribution of scores e) generally
take predictable forms

7.   If the number of events favoring A is 20 and the number
favoring non-A is 100, p(A) equals:

a) 0.20   b) 2.00 c) 0.25 d) 0.80 e) 0.17

8. If the number of events favoring A is 10 and the number favoring non-A is 5, p(A) equals:

a) 0.67 b) 2.00 c)   0.40 d)   0.67 e)   0.33

9. The question, "What is the probability that four students drawn at random from the student body will have blue eyes?" involves:

a) probabilities that cannot be ascertained   b)   the classic approach to probability   c) the empirical approach to probability   d) probabilities that are less than 0.00   e) none of the preceding

10. If one is selecting a single card from a well-shuffled deck of playing cards, the probability of obtaining a 5 is:

a) 5/52 b) 1/12 c) 1/13 d) 5/ 47 e) none of the above

11. The probability of selecting a king or a queen from a well-shuffled deck of playing cards equals:

a) 1/13 b) 2/11 c) 2/13 d) 1/12 e) 1/169

12. The probability of selecting a face card (jack, queen, or king) from a well-shuffled deck of playing card is:

a) 3/52 b) 1/2197 c) 3/ 13 d) 17/52 e) none of the preceding

13. We toss a pair of unbiased dice. The probability of obtaining a sum of 11 on the faces of the dice equals:(Recall that it is possible to obtain a 5 on the first die and 6 on the other as well as 6 on the first die and 5 on the other)

a) 1/16 b) 1/3 c) 1/35 d) 1/18 e) 1/36

14. Given a normally distributed variable with a mean equal to 100 and a standard deviation equal to 16, what is the probability of randomly drawing a score equal to or greater than 80?

a) 0.1056 b) 39.44 c) 0.3944 d) 0.8944 e) 10.56

15.   Given a normally distributed variable with a mean equal to 500 and a standard deviation equal to 100, what it the probability of randomly drawing a score as rare as 630, i.e., 630 or greater?

a) 0.9032   b) 0.0968   c) 0.4032   d) 0.130   e) 0.1936

16. Probabilities vary from:

a) - 1.00 to + 1.00 b) 0.50 to +1.00   c) 0.00 to +1.00   d) 0 to -1.00   e) none of the preceding

17. If $p = 0.15$, the chance that an event will occur are:

a) 15 in 100 b) 15 out 1000 c) almost certain d) slightly better than 1 in 100   e) about 50/50

18. Given $\mu = 50$ and $\sigma = 5$, the probability of randomly selecting an individual with a score of 40 or less is:

a) 0.45   b) 0.05   c) -2.00 d) 0.975 e) 0.0228

19. On the basis of chance, the probability of randomly selecting a case between $z = -.50$ and $z = -1.00$ is approximately:

a) 5 in 100   b) 15 in 100 c) 20 in 100   d) 34 in one hundred   e) 53 in 100

20. Sixty percent of the students in a given university come from families with annual incomes of $50,000 or more. Ninety percent of all the students have group Rorschach scores that are in the range of well-adjusted individuals. If family income and personality adjustment are uncorrelated variables, approximately what percent of students are "rich neurotics"?

a) 6 b) 10 c)   30 d) 40 e) 54

21. Given a normally distributed variable with a mean equal to 200 and a standard deviation equal to 6, what is the probability of randomly drawing a score equal to or greater than 170?

a) 0 .02266 b) 0.7734 c) 0.2734   d) 0.3011 e)   0.7266

ANSWERS   1) c; 2) e; 3) c; 4) e; 5) a; 6) e; 7) e; 8) d; 9) c; 10) c; 11) c; 12) c;   13) d; 14) d;   15) b; 16) c;   17) a; 18) e;   19) b; 20) a   21) b

9

Introduction to Inferential Statistics

Behavioral Objectives

1. Explain the purpose of sampling and the relationship of a sample to the population.

2. Define and give the function of sampling distributions.

3. Specify the two cutoff points commonly used as the basis for inferring the operation of nonchance factors. Define the alpha (α) and beta (β) levels.

4. Specify the null and alternative hypotheses and describe their role in testing statistical hypotheses. Distinguish between directional and nondirectional hypotheses.

5. State the relationship between probability and accepting and rejecting the null hypothesis in terms of indirect proof.

6. Identify two types of potential errors when rejecting and failing to reject the null and alternative hypotheses.

Chapter Review

We have previously examined the concept of sampling. In this chapter we shall explore the use of probability to generalize from samples to populations, including the testing of hypotheses and examining the errors that might be made when deciding whether or not a hypothesis is valid with respect to a given population.

Fundamental to statistical inference is the practice of drawing a sample from a population being examined. If the population parameters were readily available, there would be no reason to sample or to formulate hypotheses about the parameters. All questions about the population could be answered merely by looking at the exact values. However, since the parameters of most populations cannot be measured, we must rely on the techniques of sampling.

As you might expect, there is some inescapable inaccuracy when estimating parameters from samples. If you were to take ten different samples from a population, the chances are high that you would obtain ten different means and standard deviations.

Perhaps a few would differ sharply from one another on measures of central tendency and/or dispersion.

Suppose we were to draw all possible samples of $N = 15$ from a population. We could then calculate what is called the sampling distribution of some statistic in which we are interested. Formally defined, a sampling distribution is a theoretical probability distribution of all possible values of some sample statistic that would occur if we were to draw all possible samples of a fixed size from a given population.

To clarify the concept of a sampling distribution, let's look at a small population. Draw all possible samples of $N = 2$ from that population and construct a frequency distribution of the means. We shall assume the population includes only five values: 1, 2, 3, 4, 5. All possible means are shown in boldface within the table below. For example, if 2 is selected on the first draw (column 1, row 1) and 1 is selected on the second draw (row 1, column 1), the mean is $(2 + 1) / 2 = 3/2 = 1.5$:

	1	2	3	4	5	
1	**1.0**	**1.5**	**2.0**	**2.5**	**3.0**	$\mu = 3$
2	**1.5**	**2.0**	**2.5**	**3.0**	**3.5**	
3	**2.0**	**2.5**	**3.0**	**3.5**	**4.0**	$\sigma = 1.41$
4	**2.5**	**3.0**	**3.5**	**4.0**	**4.5**	
5	**3.0**	**3.5**	**4.0**	**4.5**	**5.0**	

$\overline{X}$	f	$f\overline{X}$	$f\overline{X}^2$	p
5	1	5	25	.04
4.5	2	9	40.5	.08
4	3	12	48	.12
3.5	4	14	49	.16
3.0	5	15	45	.20
2.5	4	10	25	.16
2.0	3	6	12	.12
1.5	2	3	4.5	.08
1.0	1	1	1.0	.04
$\Sigma f = N_{\overline{X}} = 25$		$\Sigma f\overline{X} = 75$	$\Sigma f\overline{X}^2 = 250$	$\Sigma p = 1.00$

The frequency and probability distribution of the sample means are shown on the preceding page.

Note that, since we are treating the five scores as a population from which all possible sample of N = 2 have been drawn, the mean of the sample means equals the mean of the population, $\overline{X}_{\overline{X}}$ = 75/ 25 = 3.00. Note also that we can calculate the standard deviation of the sample means. This standard deviation is known as the standard error of estimate of the mean as it represented as s_{est}. It is calculated in precisely the same way as any standard deviation. In other words,

$$s_{est} = \sqrt{SS_{\overline{X}} / N_{\overline{X}}}.$$
$$= \sqrt{25/ 24*} = 1.02$$

The standard error of estimate based on a sample size of 2 is less than the standard deviation of the population. We may generalize; As we increase the N of a sample, we lower the size of the standard error of estimate.

One further point. If we select a sample of 1 from the population of 5 scores, the probability of selecting any score is 0.20. However, the probability distribution reveals a different set of probabilities for selecting sample means based on a sample size of 2. Note, for example, the probability of selecting a sample mean of 1 or 5 is extremely low — 0.04 to be precise. If our sample size had been 3, the probability of selecting a mean of 1 or 5 would have been 0.008 (.2 X .2 X .2 = 0.008), or less that 1 in 100.

Now let us suppose the situation was more realistic— we did not know the true population values. However, imagine that we had prior evidence that the mean was equal to about 3 and the standard error of estimate was 1.02. Using the familiar z-score, we calculate the two tailed probability of obtaining a sample mean ≥ 5 or ≤ 1. Thus, z = (5 - 3)/ 1.02 = 1.96 (the pos-

* In inferential statistics, the standard deviation is based on an unbiased estimate of the population variance and uses N - 1 instead of N in the denominator. More will be said about this in later chapters.

itive value) and $z = (1-3)/1.02 = z = -1.96$ (the negative value). Looking at the standard normal curve, we see that the area equal to or beyond a z of ± 1.96 is $0.0250 + 0.0250 = 0.0500$. Note how closely this value approximates the probability of 0.04 calculated when we knew the population values with precision. But without this information, would we feel confident that a sample mean of 5 or 1 was drawn at random from a population with a true mean equal to 3? Could the difference in means be due to chance or might they represent a real difference due to nonchance factors? Stated another way, "At what point can we be reasonably confident that our sample does *not* represent chance variation?" Most social scientists have adopted one or the other of two probability levels as the cutoff point between asserting chance or nonchance factors:

1. 0.05 significance or alpha (α) level. If the event would occur 5% of time by chance, then the observed event can be attributable to nonchance or experimental factors.

2. 0.01 significance or alpha (α) level. If the probability associated with the occurrence of the event is 1 percent or less, then the results are caused by nonchance factors.

When selecting p-values to test for the significance of an event, we are usually dealing with two-tails of the distribution and the p-value should reflect both. In effect, we are interested in obtaining a p-value as rare or rarer than the event being assessed. Thus, the two-tailed p-value at $\alpha = 0.05$ would require .025 or less at both tails of the distribution. the one tailed p-value would involve 5 percent or less of the distribution at the end of the distribution specified by the researcher.

But how do researchers go about proving the hypothesis they want to test? First, we must recall that a scientific hypothesis can never be proved; at best, it can be supported. There are two hypotheses formulated:

1.The null hypothesis (H_0), which asserts no effect of the experimental conditions.

2.The alternative hypothesis (H_A), which asserts an effect of the experimental conditions.

The alternative hypothesis can be "proved" only by rejecting the null hypothesis, and this is done only when the observed outcome meets the alpha level criterion. However, failure to reject the alternative hypothesis does not mean that we have proved the null hypothesis. If we have failed to prove that something is harmful, we have not proved that it is safe.

As you can see, our chances of error are greater than you might think. Either we can reject the null hypothesis when it is actually true (type I or type α error) or we can fail to reject the null hypothesis when it is actually false (type II or type β error).

SELF TEST: MULTIPLE CHOICE

1. The population of all possible outcomes resulting from tossing a pair of hypothetical dice is:

a) finite b) very large c) relatively difficult to know conclusively d) unlimited e) none of the preceding

2. Populations:

a) can rarely be studied b) may be estimated from samples c) are often hypothetical d) are the same as samples e) none of the preceding

3. If the voting preferences of 100 registered voters in the previous national election are polled, our primary interest is in:

a) determining how they will vote   b) determining voting preferences of all registered voters   c) estimating voting preferences of individuals most likely to vote in the upcoming election d) all of the preceding e) none of the preceding

4.   If you were to draw a large number of samples from a designated population, you would not be surprised to discover:

a) some differences among the sample statistics b) a distribution of sample means arranged around some central value c) that many means differ from the hypothetical population mean d) all of the preceding e) none of the preceding

5. The statement, "The obtained result would have occurred by chance 5 percent of the time or less," employs:

a) $\alpha = 0.05$ b) the 5 percent significant level   c)   the 0.05 significance level   d) all of the above   e) none of the above

6. If we reject a true null hypothesis, we make:

a) a type I error   b) a type II error   c) a true statement   d) a type β error e) none of the preceding

7.   The alternative hypothesis always states:

a) a specific value   b) a value that can prove the null hypothesis c) a value that can lead to a type II error   d) a value that can be accepted as a result of the rejection of the null hypothesis   e) none of the preceding.

8.   Since populations can rarely be studied in total, we are interested in making inferences from:

a) Type I errors   b) samples   c) reasonable hunches   d) type II errors   e) all of the preceding.

9. With $\alpha = 0.01$, we are more willing to risk a type I error than with:

a) $\alpha = 0.01$ b) $\alpha = 0.005$ c) $\alpha = 0.025$ d) $\alpha = 0.10$ e) none of the preceding

10.   The rejection of H_0 is always:

a) direct   b) based on the rejection of H_1 c) an inference   d) based on the acceptance of H_1 e) none of the preceding

11. In a carefully conducted experiment, we obtain a p-value of 0.02. Using $\alpha = 0.05$, we would conclude:

a) the p-value is not sufficiently low to reject the null hypothesis b) the p-value is too high to reject the null hypothesis   c) the p-value is sufficiently low to reject the null hypothesis   d) the alpha level is too high to reject the null hypothesis   e) none of the preceding

12. In a carefully conducted experiment, we obtain a p-value of 0.06. Using $\alpha = 0.05$, we would conclude:

a) the p-value is sufficiently low to reject the null hypothesis b) the p-value is too high to reject the null hypothesis c) the p-value is sufficiently low to reject the alternative hypothesis d) the alpha level is too low to reject the null hypothesis e) none of the preceding

Exercises 13 - 14 are based on the following probability distribution:

Sample Mean	Probability
8	0.02
7	0.12
6	0.20
5	0.28
4	0.20
3	0.12
2	0.02

13. If a two-tailed test at alpha equals .05, which of the following means would lead to the rejection of the null hypothesis?

a) 4 or 6 b) 2 or 8 c) 7 or 2 d) 5 or 8 e) 3

14. If a one-tailed test at alpha equals 0.01, which of the following means could lead to the rejection of the null hypothesis?

a) 2 b) 5 c) 8 d) either 2 or 8 e) none of the preceding

Answers 1) d; 2) d; 3) c ; 4) d; 5) d; 6) a; 7) d; 8) b; 9) b; 10) c; 11) c; 12) b; 13) b; 14) e

10

Testing Significance of Single Samples

Behavioral Objectives

1.   State the similarities between the distribution of a sample and the distribution of a sample statistic. Explain the relationship between the size of N, the shape of the population, and the properties of the distribution of sample means.

2.   Given that the parameters of a population are known, describe the procedure for determining the probability of describing a specific sample mean. Define critical regions and their relationship to statistical hypotheses.

3.   Define point estimates. Explain their function for populations with unknown parameters. Distinguish between biased and unbiased estimates of parameters.

4.   Identify those distributions that permit the testing of hypotheses   with samples drawn from normally distributed populations in which σ is unknown. Given the z-statistic, write the ratio for the t-statistic. Define and calculate degrees of freedom.

5.   Specify the various characteristics of the t-distributions. What are the critical values?

6.   Distinguish between point estimation and interval estimation.

7.   State the relationships among critical regions, confidence intervals, and the decisions concerning the hypothetical population parameter.

8.   Describe the rationale for using a test of significance for correlation coefficients.

CHAPTER REVIEW

To begin Chapter 10, we shall continue with the subject of sampling distributions. As you should know from Figure 9.2 in the text, if the focus of our attention were the mean of a small population and we wished to consider sample sizes of 4, we would draw all possible samples of N = 4 from the population. Once we calculated the mean for each sample, the resulting distribution of means would be referred to as the sampling distribution of means. There are three characteristics of sampling distributions that are important:

1.   The mean of the sampling distribution will not vary with a change in the sample size. For example, if your overall mean of the sampling distribution of means is 10 when N = 4, it should remain 10 whether you increase your sample size to 100 or decrease it to 3. The mean of the sampling distribution of means is equal to the population mean.

2.   As you increase the sample size when drawing from a sampling distributions of means, the dispersion of sample means about the population mean will become less. Stated another way, the standard error of estimate (s_{est} or $s_{\overline{x}}$) decreases as N increases.

3.   When selected from a normal distributed population, the distribution of sample means will also be bell-shaped. This tendency will occur even when the scores in the general population are skewed, particularly as sample size increases.

Let us consider a situation that actually happens only rarely when we know the population parameters, μ and σ.

Suppose a dog trainer would like to compare the sample mean of scores for dogs presently being trained to the population mean score (65) of all the dogs previously submitted the obedience test. The question to be answered is, "What is the probability that the sample mean will significantly exceed a mean of 65?"

Before we begin our calculations, we must know the sample statistics, the population parameters, and the z-score formula to be used. We can then transform the difference between the sample and population means into a z-score. This transformation will permit us to determine areas under the normal curve.

Population mean, $\mu = 65$, $\sigma = 12$, X = 72, N = 25.

The null hypothesis is that the sample was drawn from a

population in which the mean equals 65. Since the alternative hypothesis is that the sample mean is drawn from a population in which the mean is equal to or greater than 72, a one-tailed hypothesis is being tested, using $\alpha = 0.01$. Since we are dealing with both a known population mean and a known standard deviation, z is the appropriate test statistic. First, we calculate the standard error of mean:

$$\sigma_{\overline{x}} = \sigma / \sqrt{N} = 12/5 = 2.4$$

Next comes the z-ratio

$$z = (72 - 65)/2.4 = 2.92$$

Since the test of significance is one-tailed, we look up the area equal to and beyond 2.92 in Appendix Table A. We find a probability value of .0018. This is well beyond $\alpha = 0.01$. Thus, we reject H_0 and assert the alternative hypothesis. We may conclude that the trainer's present techniques produce better performance than prior procedures.

As previously noted, we rarely know the population parameters as we did in the above hypothetical example. However, with some alterations we can still apply the same logic when the parameters are unknown. To do this, we must first estimate the population parameters from our sample data. The formula most frequently used to estimate the standard error of the mean is:

$$s_{\overline{x}} = \sqrt{SS/N(N-1)} \text{ or, alternatively, } s/\sqrt{N-1}$$

The sample mean provides the point estimate of μ.

Unlike using z as the test statistic when parameters are not known, the normal curve is not the appropriate sampling distribution. The appropriate test statistic is the t-ratio which is based on a series of distributions known as t. When N is small, the t distributions are more spread out than the standard normal distribution. However, as N increases, the t-distributions become increasingly like the normal curve.

The formula for the t-ratio is:

$$t = \frac{X - \mu_0}{s_{\overline{X}}}$$

You may have noted that, unlike the normal curve, we have been referring to multiple t-distributions rather than a single distribution. Actually, there is a family of t-distributions. Which t-distribution you should apply to a particular problem depends on the number of degrees of freedom (df). Specifically, df refers to the number of restrictions placed on a data set. The greater the number of restrictions, the fewer the degrees of freedom there are. With a single restriction, the number of degrees of freedom equal N - 1.

Just as with z-scores, we must consult a table (Table C in the appendix of the text) in deciding whether or not to reject the null hypothesis. However, instead of areas under the curve, critical values of the t-ratio are listed. To use Table C, you must know the degrees of freedom and the significance level you are using to reject H_0. The values you consult are critical values-- those values bounding the critical regions associated with the significance level you have chosen. For example, if you have 26 degrees of freedom and a significance level of 0.05 for a two-tailed test, the critical value is |2.056|. If the t-ratio you obtain is equal to or greater than |2.056|, you reject the null hypothesis and assert the alternative hypothesis.

On the other hand, if your t-ratio is less than the critical value, you may not reject the null hypothesis.

Since we are using the t-ratio to test for significance, let us examine one more area in which the same principle is applied-- the arena of correlation coefficients. When H_0 is that the correlation coefficient equal to zero, the appropriate test statistic is t, which is defined as:

$$t = \frac{r\sqrt{N-2}}{\sqrt{1 - r^2}} \qquad df = N - 2$$

Suppose we obtain an r of 0.40 with N = 27 and we use to 0.05 level, one-tailed test, to reject the null hypothesis. We find that:

$$t = (0.40 \times 25) / 0.917 = 10 / 0.917 = 10.905, \quad df = 25$$

When we look under 0.05, one tailed test and df = 25, we find a critical value of 1.708. Since the obtained value far exceeds the critical value, we reject the null hypothesis and affirm that there is a statistically significant positive correlation between the two variables.

SELF-TEST: MULTIPLE CHOICE

1.   In a normally distributed population with μ = 20, σ = 5, which of the following sample sizes will yield the smallest variation among the sample means? N equals:

a) 1 b) 5 c) 20 d) 50   e) 250

2. In a large normally distributed population with μ = 15, σ = 4, we draw samples of N = 2. Which pair of scores is *least* likely to be selected?

a) 12, 18 b) 15, 15 c) 16, 14 d) 11, 19 e) 13, 17

3. In a normally distributed population with μ = 50, σ = 10, we draw samples of N = 9. The standard error of the mean is:

a) 0.90 b) 1.11 c) 5.56 d) 3.57   e)   3.33

4. In a normally distributed population with an unknown mean, which of the following sample sizes is most likely to closely approximate μ? N equals:

 a) 1 b) 5 c) 20 d) 50   e) 250

5. That portion of the area under the curve that includes those values of a statistic that lead to the rejection of the null hypothesis is known as:

a) the law of large numbers   b) student's t-ratio   c) the critical region   d) interval estimation   e) the central limit

6. Given σ = 40, $\overline{X}$ = 210, N =1. The appropriate statistic for testing H_0: μ_0= 0, yields a value of:

a) 1.93 b) 8.20 c) 2.00 d) 16   e) 5.00

7. Given $\mu_0 = 40$ $\sigma = 10$, $\overline{X} = 50$, $z_{.01} = 2.58$. Testing H_0, we would conclude:

a) reject H_0 b)   fail to reject H_0 c) the sample mean was not drawn from a population in which $\mu = 40$ d) $\mu_0 = \mu$ e) insufficient information to answer question

8. Given: $\mu_0 = 30$ $s = 10$, $\overline{X} = 40$, N = 10, the appropriate test statistic is:

a) t   b) z   c) $\alpha = 0.05$ d) σ / N e) insufficient information to answer question

9. That portion of the area under the curve that includes those values of a statistic that lead to the rejection of the null hypothesis is known as:

a) the critical region   b) the z-ratio   c) the t statistic d) the central limit   e) all of the preceding

10.   If we were to use the z-statistic to test the null hypothesis when N is small and σ is unknown, we would :

a) increase the risk of a type I error   b) decrease the risk of a type I error   c) increase the risk of a type II error   d) both (b) and (c)   e) none of the preceding

11. Given $\mu_0 = 30$ $s = 10$, $\overline{X} = 40$, N = 10. The number of degrees of freedom is:

a) 17 b) 3   c) 39 d) 29 e) 9

12. When we specify the interval that may contain the parameter, we are stating:

a) the confidence interval   b) the crucial region   c) the α-level
d) the confidence limits   e) point estimation

13.   Which of the following is the best illustration of a null hypothesis?

a) The mean of the population is 100.   b) The mean of the sample is 100.   c) The mean of the population is not 100.   d) The mean of the sample is not 100.   e) All of the above are acceptable null hypotheses.

14.   As the sample size increases and, if the sample standard deviations remain the same, the standard error of the mean will:

a) increase b) decrease c) remain the same d) increase at first and then decrease   e)   cannot answer without knowing the sample size

15. The standard deviation of a sample distribution of means is called the:

a) sample standard   b) standard difference of the sample   c) standard error of the mean   d)   sample deviation of errors e) standard mean of the difference

16.   Assume a distribution in which s = 6. What is the standard error of the mean based on samples in which N = 10?

a)   167 b) 3.16 c) 1.5 d) 2.00 e) 1.5

17.   The t-distributions are:

a) the same as the standard normal curve   b) symmetrical   c) positively skewed   d) bimodal   e) none of the preceding

Answers 1) e; 2) d; 3) e; 4) e; 5) c; 6) c; 7) e; 8) a; 9) a; 10) a; 11) e; 12) a; 13) a; 14) b; 15) c; 16) d; 17) d

11

Statistical Inference: Two Sample Case

Behavioral Objectives

1.   Distinguish between the sampling distribution of sample means and the sampling distribution of the difference between means. Specify the parameters of the sampling distribution of the difference between means in relation to the population mean.

2. Define when the z-statistic can be used with the sampling distribution of the difference between means? State the formula for the unbiased estimates of the standard error, $\sigma_{\bar{x}_1-\bar{x}_2}$, when $N_1 \neq N_2$.

3.   If the population standard deviations are unknown, identify the statistics and the formula for testing the hypotheses about the difference between means. Know how to calculate the degrees of freedom that are associated with such a test.

4.   Describe the three assumptions underlying the use of the t-distributions. Explain the procedure to follow to test for the homogeneity of variance.

5. Identify the three factors reflected in the subject's score on the dependent variable. Explain the purpose of using correlated samples designs.

6.   Explain the before-after design and the matched group design and the advantages and disadvantages of using matched groups in reference to the standard error of the difference between means. Explain how the magnitude of r influences the standard error.

7. Given the direct difference method of calculating the student's t-ratio, identify $\overline{D}$ and $s_{\overline{D}}$. Identify the formula for t.

CHAPTER REVIEW

In Chapter 10, we looked at testing hypotheses concerning a single sample. In the present chapter, we shift our focus to a frequently used procedure, namely testing of hypotheses when two samples are involved.

Just as with the one sample case, our two sample significance testing requires null hypothesis, an alternative hypothesis that includes directional and nondirectional differences, a statistical test (such as the t-statistic), the selection of a significance level, a sampling distribution of means, and a critical region of rejection of the null hypothesis. With a discussion of a few minor adjustments in the steps as a results of two sample testing, the procedures of the one sample case are readily transferable to the two-sample case. However, in essence the approach is nearly identical.

When we are formulating hypotheses in the two sample case, our definition of the standard error of the means differs from the one sample standard error. With two samples, not only may sample size vary (N_1 does not have to equal N_2), but we draw a large number of *pairs of samples* rather than a large number of single samples, Recall that both members of each pair do not have to be equal in size. When we obtain a distribution of the difference in the means of each pair of samples, this distribution is the sampling distribution of the difference between means. In other words, with two samples, our sampling distribution is not one of sample means but, rather, a distribution of the difference between pairs of sample means.

The standard deviation of the sampling distribution between differences is called the standard error of the difference between means and is designated by $s_{\bar{X}_1 - \bar{X}_2}$ The symbol reflects the fact that we are dealing with the standard deviation of the distribution of the differences between pairs of means, The most convenient definition of the standard error of the differences in means is as follows:

$$s_{\overline{x}_1 - \overline{x}_2} = \sqrt{[(SS_1 + SS_2)/(N_1 + N_2 - 2)] \times [(1/N_1 + 1/N_2)]}$$

If the Ns in both sample are equal, the formula for the standard error of the differences between means simplifies to:

$$s_{\overline{x}_1 - \overline{x}_2} = \sqrt{\frac{SS_1 + SS_2}{N_1(N_2 - 1)}}$$

The application of the t-ratio in the two-sample case is almost identical to the use of the t-ratio in the one-sample case. The essential change is that the standand error of the difference between means is substituted in the denominator for the standard error of the means. Thus, the t-ratio is as follows:

$$t = \frac{\overline{X} - \mu_0}{s_{\overline{x}_1 - \overline{x}_2}}$$

The application of the t-ratio in the two-sample case is identical to its use in problems with single samples. In order to test hypotheses at various significance levels, two-sample case, you must determine the degrees of freedom, the t-ratio, and whether you have a two-tailed or a one-tailed alternative hypo-thesis. When you have two samples, you must subtract a single degree of freedom for each sample. In other words, you have a single restriction for each sample. Thus, df $= N_1 + N_2 - 2$. If $N_1 = 10$ and $N_2 = 12$, then df $= 22 - 2 = 20$.

Let us apply the material we have covered to a problem involving two samples, A researcher wishes to explore an allega-tion that male engineers earn more than females engineers in the

Male engineers Salary in thousands of dollars		Female Engineers Salary in thousands of dollars	
X_1	X^2_1	X_2	X^2_2
27	729	43	1849
47	2209	37	1369
28	784	26	676
49	2401	60	3600
52	2704	35	1225
38	1444	46	2116
63	3969	24	576
30	900	40	1600
56	3136		
59	3481		
Sum 449	21757	311	13011

Mean of men = 44.9   Mean of women = 38.88

SS_1 = 1596.9 SS_2 = 920.875

Mean difference   = 44.90 - 38.88 = 6.02

Standard error of the difference = $\sqrt{(1596 + 920.875) / 16)(1/10 + 1/8)}$ = 5.95

t-ratio = 6.02 / 5.95 **= 1.012**, df = 10 + 8 - 2 = 16

same occupational categories. Since we are testing a directional hypothesis that the population mean salary of male engineers is greater than the population mean salary of female engineers, our null hypothesis reads: $\mu_1 \leq \mu_2$.

In the alternative hypothesis, we wish to test not only the hypothesis that the means belong to different populations but also the that $\mu_1 > \mu_2$; in other words, the mean salary of male engineers is greater than that of female engineers.   We use a directional test of the null hypothesis at $\propto$ = 0.05.

The t-ratio is found to be 1.02. Referring to Table C in the statistical appendix we find that the one-tailed critical value at the 0.05 level at df = 16 is 1.746. Since the obtained t is not in the critical region, we fail to reject the null hypothesis. The mean difference in the salaries of female and male engineers is not statistically significant. We cannot conclude that the two groups are drawn from different populations of salaries. Note that the study is not a true experiment since it involved the comparison of intact groups (males vs females).

SELF-TEST MULTIPLE CHOICE

1.   Which of the following is *not* an acceptable statement of a null hypothesis?

a)   Among registered voters, the proportion of Democrats is greater than among Republicans. b) The mean I.Q. of the population is 106.   c) The difference between the two sample means is 0.   d) The two samples were drawn from the same population. e) The two samples were drawn from two populations with a mean difference of 2.00.

2. An experimenter randomly assigns 9 people to an experimental group and 9 other people to a control group thereby assuring the independence of the two groups.   How many degrees of freedom are there in the experimenter's t-test?

a) 18 b) 8 c) 9   d) 17   e) 16

3. Which of the following values must one know in order to test the null hypothesis based on the difference between means?

a) the mean of the population from which the samples are drawn b) the population N   c) the correlation between the sample means   d) the variability of the sample means   e) the standard deviation of the population

4.   The mean of the difference between pairs of sample means drawn at random from the same normally distributed population is:

a) 0.00   b) either $z = +1.00$ or $z = -1.00$ c)   greater than $z = +2.85$ or less than -2.58 d) unknown because the difference depends directly on the σ of the population e) the definition of the standard error of the mean

5.   Which of the following is *not* an assumption underlying the t-test?

a) normality b) random sampling c) homogeneity of variance d)   unbiased estimate of the population variance   e) discrete scales underlying measurement

6.   If we say that there is a real difference between the mean of two conditions but in reality there is no difference, we have committed what type of error?

a) type I error b) type II error c) type III error d) beta error e) two-tailed error

7.   Which of the following could not serve as a null hypothesis in the two-sample case?

a) $\mu_1 - \mu_2 = 0$ b) $\mu_1 - \mu_2 = 5$ c) $\mu_1 - \mu_2 = -5$ d) $\overline{X}_1 - \overline{X}_2 = 0$ e) none of the preceding

8.   Which of the following is a true statement?

a) The t-distributions are symmetrical about a mean of 1.00. b) We accept H_0 when we obtain a negative t-ratio. c) The t-ratio is used only when the standard deviation of each population is known.   d) The t-distributions are symmetrical about a difference in means of 0.00. e) None of the preceding are true statements.

Questions 9 through 12 refer to the following information:

$\overline{X}_1 = 100$ $\overline{X}_2 = 110$ $N_1 = 10$

$SS_1 = 79.6$ $SS_2 = 79.6$ $N_2 = 10$

9. $s_{\overline{x}_1 - \overline{x}_2}$ equals:

a) 1.20 b) 1.33 c) 4.00   d) 5.66 e) 10.00

10. The t-ratio for testing H_0: $\mu_1 = \mu_2$ equals:

a) 1.000 b) 1.767   c) 2.500 d) 7.519 e) 8.333

11. The degrees of freedom equals:

a) 8 b) 9 c) 10   d) 18 e) 19

12. Employing $\alpha = 0.05$, one tailed test, you would conclude that:

a) the obtained t-ratio does not fall within the critical region   b) the obtained $t > t_{0.05}$ c) there was no significant difference between the means   d) the null hypothesis was accepted e) the null hypothesis was rejected a the 0.05 level.

13.   If we randomly draw pairs of samples of a fixed N from a population in which $\mu = 78$, $\sigma = 10$ and construct a frequency distribution of differences between pairs, we would expect $\mu_{\bar{x}_1 - \bar{x}_2}$ to equal approximately:

a) 78.00   b) 10.00   c)   0.00 d)   7.80   e) cannot answer question without knowing N

14. If we randomly draw pairs of samples of a fixed N from a population in which $\mu_1 = 72$, $\sigma_1 = 10$ and $\mu_2 = 75$, $\sigma_{12} = 10$ and calculate the differences   between these pairs of sample means, we would expect $\mu_{\bar{x}_1 - \bar{x}_2}$ to equal approximately:

a) 0.00 b) -3.00   c) 3.00 d) .30 e) cannot answer question without knowing N

Answers 1) a; 2) e; 3) d; 4) a; 5) e; 6) a; 7) d; 8) d; 9) b; 10) d; 11) d; 12) e; 13) c; 14) b

12

An Introduction to the Analysis of Variance

Behavioral Objectives

1. What is the purpose of the one-way analysis of variance (ANOVA)

2. Define and distinguish between the within-group variance and the between-group variance. What is their relationship to the magnitude of the F-ratio?

3.   Explain how the total sum of squares, the between-group sum of squares, and the within-group sum of squares are derived. What is the relationship among them?

4. How are the variance estimates, the degrees of freedom, and the F-ratio obtained? Describe exactly what the null hypothesis states concerning the variance estimates and the F-ratio.

5. What is the underlying assumption of analysis of variance?

6. How does a one-way correlated ANOVA differ from the one-way independent-samples ANOVA?

7.   State the possible advantages and disadvantages of correlated-samples ANOVA (between-subjects, within-subjects) from an independent-samples ANOVA.

CHAPTER REVIEW

Just as the t-ratio is commonly used as a test of the null hypothesis in the two-sample case, the analysis of variance is the test of choice for multigroup comparisons. Researchers in the behavioral sciences have become increasingly involved with experimental designs that involve several levels of a single variable or even two or more variables. More complex designs require the use of the analysis of variance. In this review, we shall focus our attention on the multigroup case with a single independent variable.

The analysis of variance is a statistical technique that enables the investigator to assess differences among many groups.

As in the preceding chapters, the familiar sum of squares concept plays an invaluable role in the analysis of variance. As its name suggests, the analysis of variance provides a method for comparing groups differences on the basis of different variance estimates that they provide. To do so, we make repeated use of various sum of squares. To illustrate the calculation in a simple three group ANOVA, we'll use the uncomplicated data set shown below:

Group 1	Squares of 1	Group 2	Squares of 2	Group 3	Squares of 3
2	4	3	9	7	49
4	16	5	25	9	81
5	25	8	64	11	121
11	45	16	98	27	251

$$\Sigma X_{tot} = (11 + 16 + 27) = 54$$

$$SS_1 = 45 - 121/3 \qquad SS_2 = 98 - 256/3 \qquad SS_3 = 251 - 729/3$$
$$= 45 - 40.33 \qquad = 98 - 85.33 \qquad = 251 - 243$$
$$= 4.67 \qquad = 12.67 \qquad = 8$$

$$N_1 = 3 \qquad N_2 = 3 \qquad N3 = 3 \qquad N_{tot} = 9$$

$$SS_w = SS_1 + SS_2 + SS_3 = 25.34$$

As you can see, the within-group sum of squares equals 25.34.

The formula for calculating the between-group sum of squares is :

$$SS_{bet} = (\Sigma X_1^2 / N_1 + \Sigma X_2^2 / N_2 + \Sigma X_3^2 / N_3) - (\Sigma X_{tot})^2 / N_{tot}$$

$$= (40.33 + 85.33 + 243) - (54)^2 / 9$$
$$= 368.66 - 324 = 44.66$$

The formula for calculating the total sum of squares is familiar. It is the sum of the squares of the variable minus the sum of the variable squared and divided by N. Thus,

$$SS_{tot} = 45 + 98 + 251 - 324$$
$$= 394 - 324 = 70$$

$$SS_w + SS_{bet} = 25.34 + 44.66 = 70.00$$

Since the total sum of squares is divided into two components—the between SS and the within SS, these two components must add up to the total SS. If not, an error has been made. As you can see, both total sum of squares are the same.

The variance estimates of the between group and the within group sums of squares are found by dividing each quantity by the appropriate number of degrees of freedom. For the between group sum of squares, the degrees of freedom equal the number of cells minus one. The formula is:

$$df_{bet} = k - 1$$

where k equals the number of cells.

For the within-groups, the degrees of freedom equal the total N of the combined groups minus the number of cells.

$$df_W = N - k$$

In the preceding example, $df_W = 9 - 3 = 6$.

For significance testing in ANOVA, we use the F-ratio, i.e., the ratio of variances. In the analysis of variance, the F-ratio is defined as the unbiased variance estimate $(\hat{s}^2_{bet})$ divided by the unbiased estimate of the within group variance estimate ($\hat{s}^2_W$).

$$F = \hat{s}^2_{bet} / \hat{s}^2_W$$

For both these variance estimates, we merely divide the appropriate sum of squares by the corresponding degrees of freedom.

Using the information that has presented so far, let's construct a summary table of the sum of squares, degrees of freedom, estimated variance, and the F-ratio.

Summary Table

Variable	Sum of squares	df	Estimated Variance	F-ratio
Between	44.66	2	22.33	
Within	25.34	6	4.22	5.29
Total	70.00	8		

The null hypothesis states that the two independent variance estimates may be regarded as estimates of the same population value. Symbolically speaking,

$$H_0: \mu_1 = \mu_2 = \mu_3 = \cdots \mu_k$$

Is our F-ratio significant at the 0.05 level? Since we have three groups in our example, $H_0: \mu_1 = \mu_2 = \mu_3$ and F-ratio of 5.29, we look for the critical value in Table D at 2 and 6 degrees of freedom. We find it to be equal to or greater than 5.14. Since our obtained F exceeds this critical value, we reject the null hypothesis and assert the alternative hypothesis.

The preceding illustration was based on a one-way ANOVA in which there are two or more levels or categories of a single treatment variable. The statistical analysis is designed to test the null hypothesis that the different levels or categories were drawn from the same population. Rejection of the null hypothesis permits us to conclude that the population means from which the samples were drawn are not the same. Therefore, we can conclude that the independent variable exercised a selective effect over the dependent measure.

In Chapter 11, we compared and contrasted two-group independent sample t-tests with two-group correlated sample t-tests. Recall both the advantages and the disadvantages of the use of correlated samples (matched pairs or before-after measures on the same subjects). The randomized block one-way ANOVA is an extension of these procedures to designs involving more than two treatments of a single variable and shares both the advantages and disadvantages, namely:

Advantages	**Disadvantages**
Assures investigator that each is equivalent on the initial ability level of the independent variable since both members of a pair are roughly equivalent.	There is a loss of degrees of freedom. If the correlation is zero or negligible, the error term is not reduced but a higher value on the test statistic is required for significance.
A source of random error is identified and quantified, thus permitting a corresponding reduction in the error term. A more precise estimate of the treatment effects results.	During the study, for each loss of a member of a matched pair (or a single subject in a before-after design), we lose two observations. High attrition rates can undermine the goals of a study.

The partitioning of the sum of squares in a one-way correlated measures ANOVA may be diagramed as below. As a point of fact, what would be the within-group sum of squares in an independent squares design has been partitioned into two components: block SS and residual SS. The residual SS is not usually calculated directly, since blocks SS and the between-group sum of squares can be subtracted from the total SS to yield the residual SS, which is used to calculate the error term.

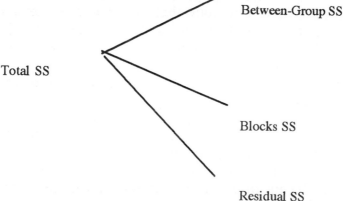

Between-Group SS

Total SS

Blocks SS

Residual SS
(for error term)

SELF-TEST: MULTIPLE CHOICE

1. In a simple analysis of variance, the assumption of homogeneity of variance applies to:

a) the variance within the treatment groups   b) the variance of the means associated with the treatment groups   c) the total variance   d) all of the above   e) none of the above

2. When a variable is "confounded" in an experiment, it means that:

a) it must be varied systematically b) it must be randomized with respect to subjects   c) it cannot be analyzed as a separate source of variance d) the treatments are contaminated   e) all of the preceding

3. The independent variable in analysis of variance:

a) must be correlated   b) may be nominal scales c) must be at least interval scales d) should be ratio scales   e) should not be ordinal scales

4. If you obtained an F-ratio equal to 1.04 with df = 2/20. you could legitimately conclude that:

a) there were no significant differences among the means   b) you had made an error   c) you had proved that the variances were equal d) the null hypothesis was proved   e) all of the preceding

5. If the means for each of the treatment groups were identical, the F-ratio would be:

a) 1.00   b) zero c) a positive number between 0 and 1   d) a negative number e) infinite

6. To obtain the between-group variance estimate, you divide the between-group sum of squares by:

a) N-1df b) Ndf c) k - 1   d) within-group sum of squares e) within-group variance estimate

7. In the analysis of variance two sample case

a) the F-ratio yields the same probability values as the t-ratio   b) $F = t^2$ c) $t = \sqrt{F}$ d) $df_{bet} = 1$ e) all of the preceding

8.   The between-group variance estimate:

a) is associated with $df = N - k$ b) reflects the magnitude of the differences between and/or among the means   c) is analogous to the standard error of the mean in the t-ratio   d) is referred to as the error term e) none of the preceding

9.   In multigroup experimental designs, a disadvantage of restricting our statistical analyses to individual comparisons between pairs of experimental conditions is that:

a) the statistical work is tedious b) the risk of a Type II error is increased   c)   the risk of a Type I error is increased   d) all of the preceding e) none of the preceding

10.   For a given number of degrees of freedom, as the variability among means increases relative to the variability within groups:

a) The F-ratio is unaffected   b) the F-ratio increases   c) the F-ratio decreases   d) the risk if a Type-I error increases   e) cannot answer without knowing the total N

11. In multigroup comparisons, if we were to subtract a constant from all scores, the resulting F-ratio would:

a) increase   b) decrease   c) remain the same   d) change in an unpredictable fashion   e) cannot answer without knowing the value of the constant

Answers   1) a; 2) c;   3) c;   4) a;   5) b;   6) c;   7) e;   8) b; 9) c;   10) b;   11) c

13

Nonparametric Tests
of Significance

Behavioral Objectives

1. What are the necessary conditions to use the normal approximation of binomial values?

2. Why has the χ^2 test been described as a "goodness of fit" technique in the single-variable case?   What is the null hypothesis for the χ^2 test?   State the formula for finding the degrees of freedom in the one-variable case?

3. In the two-variable case of the χ^2 test, specify how the expected frequency for each cell is obtained. What is the formula for the degrees of freedom in this case?

4. Know what the assumptions of independence of observations in the χ^2 test are and what happens when these assumptions are violated.

5. When is the Mann-Whitney U-test the appropriate statistical test? What does the null hypothesis predict about the values of U and U'?   Specify the relationship between the obtained values of U and U' and the tables values found in Tables I_1 and I_4.   Identify the various notations used to determine the values of U and U'.

6. What conditions are necessary for using the sign test? What does the null hypothesis predict in the direction of changes in paired scores? State the advantages of the sign test.

7. List the conditions that are necessary for selecting the Wilcoxon matched-pairs signed-rank test. State the underlying assumptions of the signed-rank test.

CHAPTER REVIEW

At times researchers may question whether their data meet the assumptions underlying a parametric test of significance. On these occasions, they may look for a nonparametric test of significance. as an alternative test to their parametric counterpart. In this chapter, we examine several nonparametric tests that serve as alternative tests to their parametric counterparts.

When dealing with nominally scaled data, the binomial test may be applied to two-category variables, and the χ^2 test is appropriate for tests of significance when there are more than two values of the nominally scaled variable. For example, if we wish to test the null hypothesis of a given divorce rate within a given population, the binomial test may be used for relatively small randomly selected samples. Recall that in a two-category population, the relationship between P and Q —the proportion of cases within each of two categories — is defined by Q = 1 - P or P = 1- Q. When there are only two categories, it follows that if 0.80 of the cases are classified under P, then the proportion falling in the Q category equals 0.20. Let's look at a hypothetical example:

County officials in a Montana community wish to learn if the divorce rate has changed from a prior estimate of 0.10 (i.e., P = 0.10 and Q = 0.90). They decide to select a random sample of 20 marriages that have occurred since this last estimate and record the proportion of marriages ending in divorce (P) and the proportion in which the couples remained married (Q). If a change has occurred, it is probably in the direction of a higher divorce rate, i.e. P > 0.10. For this reason, a one-tailed test is justified.

With this information, let us formally state the problem and use the binomial as our test statistic.

1. H_0: $P \le 0.10$

2. H_1: $P > 0.10$

3. Statistical test: Binomial test since we are dealing with a two-category population in which P + Q = 1.00.

4. Significance level: α = 0.05, one-tailed test.

5. Sampling distribution: binomial expansion but with critical values provided in Table N of the text.

6. Critical region: All values of x that are so extreme that the probability of their occurrence under the null hypothesis is less than or equal to 0.05, one-tailed test.

Once the county officials have formally stated the problem, they randomly select 20 marriage/divorce records from their official records. They find that 14 couples are still married while 6 have been divorced. Reading down column headed by 0.10 down to N= 20, it is seen that 4 or more divorces will read to the rejection of the null hypothesis at the 0.05 level, one-tailed test. Since 6 divorces exceed the critical value of 4, we reject the null hypothesis and conclude that the divorce rate in the county has increased since the prior study.

Table N provides critical values of the binomial when $N \leq 49$. However, with larger Ns, the z-statistic based on the normal curve provides a close approximation to the binomial when NPQ ≥ 9. For example, if $N = 62$, $P = 0.6$ and $Q = 0.4$, NPQ = 14.88. Since this value is greater than 9, the normal approximation to the binomial is appropriate.

Suppose you are an entomologist who has been retained by a recently industrialized community to ascertain if increased air pollution has changed the proportion of black versus white moths inhabiting your region. Some critics of industrialization have argued that the smokier air has provided a selective protection from predation of the black moths since they blend better than the white moths with the darker background. Ten years previously, an in-depth study by a colleague found that the proportion of white moths was 0.60. Your recent study revealed that 26 of 62 moths which you observed were white. Was there a significant change over the 10-year period? Use $\alpha = 0.05$, two-tailed test.

The normal approximation to the binomial test statistic, z, requires that we determine the number of observations in the P-category, obtain the proportion NP expected under the null hypothesis and the standard error of the proportion ($\sqrt{NPQ}$):

$$ z = \frac{x - NP}{\sqrt{NPQ}} $$

In the present example, $x = 26$, $N = 62$, $P = 0.60$ and $Q = 0.40$. Applying the z-score approximation to the binomial, we obtain:

$$\frac{26 - 37.2}{\sqrt{(62)(0.60)(0.40)}} = \frac{-11.2}{3.857} = -2.90$$

In Table A in the appendix of the text, we find that the area beyond z = -2.90 equals 0.0019. The two-tailed value, then, is 2 X 0.0019 = 0.0038. This clearly exceeds the .05 significance level. Thus, we may reject the null hypothesis and conclude that the proportion of white to black moths has decreased over the past 10 years. Note, however, that this is not a true experiment. Other factors, such as increased pollutant levels and use of pesticides may have affected the survival of white and black moths.

The binomial test applies only to two-category situations. What statistical technique can be used when we are interested in statistical comparisons of two or more categories of a single variable? The statistic χ^2 is used under these circumstances. Since we are testing the difference between observed and expected frequencies, the test is sometimes referred to as a "goodness of fit" test.

The formula used to test the null hypothesis is as follows:

$$\chi^2 = \sum_{i=1}^{k} \frac{(f_0 - f_e)^2}{f_e}$$

where f_e = the observed frequency within a given category and $\sum_{i=1}^{k}$ directs us to sum this ratio over all k categories.

To find the degrees of in the multicategory one variable case, we may use the formula df = k - 1. If there are 10 categories, df = 10 - 1 = 9. Table B in appendix of the text is the appropriate table to consult in order to find the critical values of χ^2 at various levels of significance.

Consider the following one-variable problem in which a marketing firm is testing the acceptability of five different toys. To do so, researchers randomly select 30 potential customers for its products. Each subject is permitted to examine independently five different toys and to select the one which he or she prefers. The following table lists the results of the study.

Toy	Number Preferred	Number Expected	$(f_0 - f_e)^2 / f_e$
1	6	6	0
2	15	6	13.5
3	3	6	1.5
4	0	6	6.0
5	6	6	0

$$df = 4 \qquad N = 30 \qquad \Sigma (f_0 - f_e)^2 / f_e = 21$$

$\chi^2 = 21$ is given in the last column of the table. Note that the values in this column are obtained by subtracting and squaring the number expected for each toy from the number preferred and dividing by the number expected. Thus, for toy #2, we obtain: $(15 - 6)^2 / 6 = 81/6 = 13.5$.

With 4 degrees of freedom and a significance level of .05, we consult Table B in the appendix of the text and find that the critical value for rejecting the null hypothesis is equal to or greater than 9.488. Since the obtained value of chi square is equal to 21, we reject the null hypothesis and assert the alternative hypothesis. In other words, the five toys are not equally preferred.

We have seen that, when dealing with categorical or nominal variables, the binomial (or the z-score approximation) is appropriate when there are two categories of a single variable and chi square is suitable when there are more than two categories. But what is our choice when we are dealing with interval/ratio scales but the assumptions of the parametric tests are questionable? The Mann-Whitney U-test is called into play as an alternative to the Student t-ratio for independent samples.

Let us consider a hypothetical study in which the Mann-Whitney is the appropriate statistical test. Suppose we are comparing the self-esteem scores of 8 randomly selected males and 9 females. Note that it is not a true experiment because the Ss are not randomly assigned to "conditions." It is, rather, an intact group design.

Since the data are ordinal, we use the Mann-Whitney U rather than Student's t-ratio. Following are the results of this hypothetical study.

Male		Female	
Self-esteem	Rank	Self-esteem	Rank
15	4	8	1
21	6	10	2
32	8	12	3
40	11	19	5
49	13	25	7
50	14	34	9
52	15	36	10
65	17	48	12
		56	16
$N_1 = 8$ $R_1 = 88$		$N_2 = 9$ $R_2 = 65$	

Selecting Male as Group 1, we see that $N_1 = 8$ and $N_2 = 9$. Summing the ranks for the two groups, we find that $R_1 = 88$ and $R_2 = 65$. If we follow the formula for U, we obtain the quantity 20;

$$U = (8)(9) + \frac{(8)(9)}{2} - 88$$
$$= 72 + 36 - 88$$
$$= 20$$

Consulting Table I_1 in the text, we see that our obtained U falls within the region of nonrejection as indicated by the border values of 9 and 63. In other words, U must be equal to or less than 9 or U' be equal to or greater than 63 to reject the null hypothesis at the 0.01 level two-tailed test. Since U does not fall outside these values, we fail to reject the null hypothesis.

Suppose that our design includes matched pairs (Ss matched on the basis of their similarity on the dependent measure) but the scores are considered, at best, of ordinal measures. The first step would be to calculate the quantitative differences between pairs of scores. Our next step would be to rank these differences according to the absolute value of each difference. Note that we are ranking the differences rather than the scores.

Activity Score

Matched pair	Two days	Two weeks	Difference	Rank of difference
A	30	14	+16	+6
B	12	34	-22	-8
C	19	22	-3	-1
D	38	29	+9	+3
E	10	17	-7	-2
F	14	28	-14	-5
G	25	14	+11	+4
H	20	39	-19	-7
I	11	42	-31	-10
J	8	31	-23	-9

Sum of positive ranks =   13
Sum of negative ranks = -55

Note that the rank of the difference is assigned according to the absolute value of the difference. The sign of the difference is then placed before the rank of the difference. For example, the rank of 2 corresponds to a difference score of -7, so the negative sign is carried over to the rank of difference column. Therefore, the assigned ranking equals -2.

On the basis of the T-statistic, we make a decision as to whether to accept or reject the null hypothesis. In this case, our null hypothesis leads us to expect that the sum of the negative ranks and the positive ranks more or less balances to a value approaching 0.

To calculate T, we must determine whether the positive ranks or the negative ranks sum to a smaller **absolute value.** The smaller value becomes our T-statistic. In this example, the sum of the positive ranks equals 13 whereas the sum of the negative ranks equals -42. Since the value of the sum of positive ranks is less than the absolute ranks, our T-statistic is 13. Turning to Table J in the appendix of the textbook, we see that we require a T-value equal to or less than 8 to achieve significance at the .05 level. Since T = 13 is greater than 8, we fail to reject the null hypothesis.

SELF-TEST: MULTIPLE CHOICE

1. In a 2 X 2 chi square table, the obtained frequency for each cell is 20. Total frequency is 80. The theoretical frequency for the cell in column 1, row 1 is:

a) 40 b) 80 c) 10 d) 2 e) 20

2. The general rule of thumb for ascertaining the degrees of freedom for all contingency-type tables of r rows and c columns, where the marginal totals are used in setting up the expected frequencies (chi square) is:

a) (r - 2)(c - 1)   b) (r - 2)(c - 2)   c) (r - 1)(c-1)   d) (r)(c) - 2   e) 2(r)(c)

3. Which of the following is a nonparametric test?

 a) t b) chi-square c) z d) z for correlated samples e) none of the preceding

4. In a 1 X 6 chi square test, df =:

a) 5 b) 6 c) 0 d) 7 e) none of the preceding

5. In testing H_0 that P = Q = 1/2 for a two-category population when the sample size equals 9, we should employ:

a)   the normal approximation to binomial values   b)   the chi square test of independence c) the chi square one-variable case d) the binomial table for $P = Q = 1/2$ e) none of the preceding

6. In testing that $P = Q = 1/2$ for a two-category population when $N = 60$, we should employ:

a) the normal approximation to binomial values b) the binomial expansion c) the Student t-ratio d) the Mann-Whitney U e) none of the preceding

7. To test the null hypothesis of equal preference for three candidates who are running for the same political office, a sample of 510 registered voters is employed. What test of significance should be used?

a) the binomial expansion   b) the normal approximation of binomial values c) the chi square single-variable test d) the chi square multivariable test e) none of the preceding

8. Referring back to Exercise 7, the expected frequency under the null hypothesis for candidate B is:

a) 255 b) 340 c) 153 d) 170 e) cannot answer without knowing more about the popularity of the three candidates

9.   The approximation of the normal curve to the binomial is greatest when:

a) N is large and $P \neq Q \neq 1/2$ b) N is small and $P \neq Q \neq 1/2$ c) N is small and $P = Q = 1/2$ d) N is large and $P = Q = 1/2$ e) none of the preceding

10. Assume: two conditions, experimental and control. The N per group is 15. Subjects are assigned at random to the experimental conditions and the scale of measurement is ordinal or higher. The assumption of normality cannot be maintained. The appropriate test statistic is:

a) Student's t-ratio for uncorrelated samples   b) Wilcoxon's matched-pairs signed-rank test c) the binomial test d) Mann-

Whitney U e) correlated samples t-test

11.   Assume: two conditions, experimental and control, matched subjects, scale of measurement is ordinal in which the scores indicate the direction and the amount of the difference, and assumption of normality cannot be maintained. The appropriate test statistic is:

a)   Student's t-ratio for uncorrelated samples   b) Wilcoxon's matched-pairs signed-rank test c) the sign test d) Mann-Whitney U e) correlated samples t-ratio

12.   Assume: two conditions, experimental and control, paired samples, scale of measurement is interval or ratio, assumption of normality is valid. The appropriate test statistic is:

a)   Student's t-ratio for uncorrelated samples   b) Wilcoxon's matched-pairs signed-rank test c) the sign test d) Mann-Whitney U e) correlated samples t-ratio

13. Assume: two conditions, experimental and control, matched subjects, scale is ordinal, assumption of normality cannot be maintained. The appropriate test statistic is:

a)   Student's t-ratio for uncorrelated samples   b) Wilcoxon's matched-pairs signed-rank test c) the sign test d) Mann-Whitney U e) correlated samples t-ratio

14. Assume: two conditions, experimental and control, Ss assigned at random, scale of measurement is interval or higher, assumption of normality is valid. The appropriate test statistic is:

a)   Student's t-ratio for uncorrelated samples   b) Wilcoxon's matched-pairs signed-rank test c) the sign test d) Mann-Whitney U e) correlated samples t-ratio

15. Given $N_1 = 5$, $N_2 = 5$, $\alpha = 0.05$, two-tailed test and the critical value of $U \leq 2$ or ≥ 23, we obtain a U of 24, we should:

a) assert H_1 b) fail to reject H_0 c) depends upon whether we have obtained U or U'   d) assert H_0 e) none of the preceding

Answers   1) e; 2) c; 3) b; 4) a; 5) d 6) a; 7) c; 8) d; 9) d;
10) d; 11) b; 12) e; 13) b; 14) a; 15) a